From Darkness to Daylight

How Tri-County Electric Cooperative Brought Power to Southeast Minnesota

THE
DONNING COMPANY
PUBLISHERS

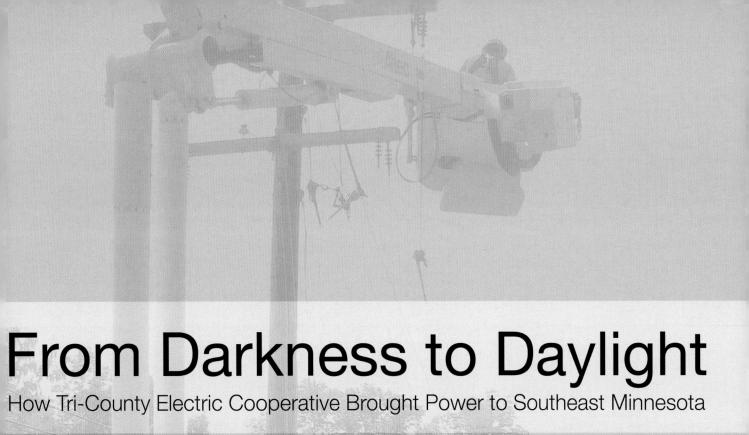

From Darkness to Daylight

How Tri-County Electric Cooperative Brought Power to Southeast Minnesota

By Jim McCarty

Photo on inside front cover: Standing (left to right): Amon Berge, Melvin Hoiseth, Vernon Burke, Norman Ebner, Sam Helleland, Ed Reishus, George James, Turkey Thompson, Carl Legwold, Ben Hasleiet, Hubert Nordness, Ed Laugen, Bill Grove, Forest Giesler, Vernon James, and Jake Gutterson. Sitting (left to right): Pete Quaman, Frank Carlson, Fred Seabright, Helmer Swensied, Harry Arnold, Alfred Lee, Martin James, Jim Baker, Herman Anderson, Meredith Haslerud, and George Ellestad.

Photo on inside back cover: Current employees of Tri-County include, front row (left to right): Andy Prinsen, Craig Cornell, Tim Anderson, Jamie Breeser, Cory Pederson, and Steve Bronner. Second row, sitting: Chad Chaffee, Annie Hoiland, Gordon Johnson, Lorraine Benson, Mary Rislove, Lori Clobes, Virginia Johnson, Audra Skalet, Susie Norby, June Vitse, Adrienne Lofgren, Sara Krage, Mary Lou Walther, Rhonda Bauer, Mike Ebner, Brenda Tesch, and Brian Krambeer. Third row: Gary Elliott, Randall Ashbacher, Allen Ziebell, Dennis LeFebvre, John DeGeorge, Tom Wittry, Brett Bergan, Dean Stoa, Jeff Hoiland, Jerome Gudmundson, Glen Jensson, Jim Culhane, Jim Steinmetz, Maynard Rustad, Kaye Bernard, Bob Spartz, and Ted Kjos. Back row: Eric Vitse, George Ingram, Keith Pederson, Brian Bauer, Steve Oian, Davin Thompson, Charlie Mueller, Matt Ginther, Steve Culhane, Troy Schiltz, Tyler Eide, Joe Jordan, and Brad Pecinovsky. Photo courtesy of Ross Himlie Photography.

The Donning Company Publishers
184 Business Park Drive, Suite 206
Virginia Beach, VA 23462

Steve Mull, General Manager
Barbara Buchanan, Office Manager
Heather L. Floyd, Editor
Chad Harper Casey, Graphic Designer
Priscilla Odango, Imaging Artist
Lori Kennedy, Project Research Coordinator
Tonya Hannink, Marketing Specialist
Pamela Engelhard, Marketing Advisor

Steve Mull, Project Director

Library of Congress Cataloging-in-Publication Data

McCarty, Jim, 1962-
  From darkness to daylight : how Tri-County Electric Cooperative brought
power to southeast Minnesota / by Jim McCarty.
     p. cm.
  ISBN 978-1-57864-656-2 (hardcover : alk. paper)
 1. Tri-County Electric Cooperative--History. 2. Electric
utilities--Minnesota--History. 3. Rural
electrification--Minnesota--History. I. Tri-County Electric Cooperative II.
Title.
  HD9685.U7T742 2011
  334--dc22
                        2010042505

Printed in the United States of America at Walsworth Publishing Company

Table of Contents

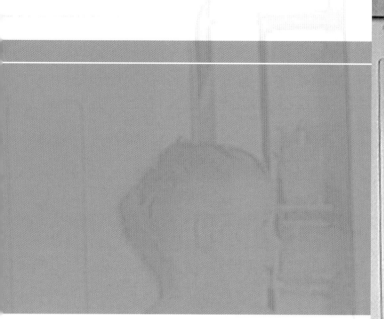

Families had a lot less spoiled milk after they received electricity from Tri-County Electric Cooperative and installed electric refrigerators.

Acknowledgments

Fully knowing this list will leave someone out, the author wishes to thank the following people for their assistance, without which this book would not have been possible:

Freddie Arnold, retired lineman for Tri-County Electric
The late Earl Johnson, retired manager for Tri-County Electric
Brenda Tesch, director of public relations for Tri-County Electric
The staff of the Minnesota Historical Society, St. Paul
Deb Mirasola and Katie Thomson, Dairyland Power Cooperative

Introduction

As the nation struggles to bring itself out of its current financial crisis, this book is being written to highlight the efforts of those who made Tri-County Electric Cooperative the success story it is today. Perhaps the story of this business, which began as a partnership between government and the people, can serve as a model for those working on solutions to today's economic woes.

It was in similar but much darker circumstances that a small group of enlightened rural people from Fillmore, Houston, and Winona counties in southeastern Minnesota took on the daunting challenge of bringing electricity to their farms and homes when so many others said it couldn't be done.

That they succeeded beyond their wildest dreams is a great testament to the American spirit, that same spirit that crossed the continent and bridged divides and never said never, even when the odds were against them. From its humble beginnings in 1936, Tri-County Electric Cooperative has grown into one of the nation's most successful electric cooperatives, building on the solid foundation established by those pioneers of rural electrification.

Over the years, the cooperative has been blessed by a strong, progressive board of directors who hired the right people for the job and supported them in their efforts. Tough decisions made turned out to be the right ones in most cases. Opportunities were seized before they could become lost. Chances were taken when the odds were right. And through it all, the leaders of this institution never forgot the ideals of its founders, especially this one:

Tri-County Electric Cooperative exists for only one reason, and that is to provide the best possible service at the lowest possible cost to its member/owners. By removing the profit motive, your electric cooperative could and still does focus on its mission of service.

Tri-County Electric's employees, board, and members worked together to overcome adversity that included storms, financial pressures, and the 2007 flood that destroyed its headquarters and equipment. But like gold tested in fire, the cooperative spirit helped the organization emerge stronger each time.

On the eve of Tri-County Electric Cooperative's seventy-fifth anniversary, it's appropriate that we take a look back at the history of this great triumph of the human condition, for it's only by learning from our past that we can achieve great things in the future. Turn the page, dear reader, and let us begin…

—Jim McCarty

Chapter 1—
Before There Was Electricity

It is very hard for a person today to imagine life without electricity, but for thousands of rural people in the 1930s, that was a reality. Days began in the dark, with the farmer fumbling for matches to light candles or a kerosene lamp in order to provide enough light to see. They ended the same way.

In the winter, most likely the fire in the woodstove had gone out overnight and those first steps out from under the down comforter were difficult ones. Water brought in from the well or a spring would have frozen solid.

Breakfast had to wait for the woman of the house to fire up the wood cook stove, which could take a long time to heat up. Meanwhile, chores had to come first anyway. The farmer trudged out of the house armed with a lantern, which shed its feeble light in a pool at his feet in a vain attempt at casting away the darkness. One unnamed dairy farmer wrote about the experience he and other farm kids shared:

"We kept a lantern hanging beside the kitchen door. Winter mornings I'd take that lantern and head for the barn. It would be so dark out you'd think you were in a box with the lid shut. We always had at least a dozen cows to milk and only me and my dad to do it.

Reading by the light of a coal oil lamp made homework a chore and eyestrain common for rural kids in the days before electricity.

Previous page: *Some area residents had power as early as 1915 thanks to this historic dam on the Root River.*

Students enjoy sledding near the one-room Rush Creek School in the days before electricity came to their school.

"I had a lot of chores to do before I went to school… that made me late to school some mornings. I'd fill the wood box beside the kitchen stove and I'd bring in a bucket of water. Sometimes the hand pump would be frozen solid and I'd have to thaw it out before I could pump the water.

"As soon as I got home from school I had chores to do and then an early supper. After that I'd get at my homework. I'd study by a kerosene lamp in the kitchen up close to the stove. We all spent most of our time in the kitchen during the winter."

Farm wife Margaret Reynolds described what life was like before electricity came to the Minnesota countryside in an article for the May 1985 *Rural Minnesota News*:

"Mornings began with starting a fire in the cook stove in order to proceed with the rest of the day's activities. The fire warmed up the kitchen, heated the water in the back reservoir, and provided a place to cook our breakfast.

"When the pails of fresh, foamy milk were carried into the back porch, it was time to start turning the handle for the cream separator, turning around, faster and faster, until the little bell began to ring and continuing at that speed until all the milk had gone through.

"An endless task in those days was that of washing the dishes and separator, the children, the floors, the laundry. I would pump water by hand into two pails, carry it from the well to the house, then pour it into a large tub on the stove to heat, all the while stuffing more wood into the firebox. When the water was hot, the washing was done by hand (no disposable diapers) and hung to dry, outside if the weather was nice, all around the inside of the house if not.

"Our refrigerator then was a deep hole in the ground with a cover on it. We put our milk, butter, and meat in pails and lowered them by rope to the cool depths below.

Above: *Hanging clothes outside—or on any available space inside when it was cold or wet— was the only option for rural homemakers.*

Left: *Herd sizes had to be small when cows were milked by hand. At many electric cooperatives, dairy farmers led the effort to bring electricity to farms.*

"There was no telephone or television. A little battery radio was our source of news and music. We read a lot of books, we played games, we talked to one another.

"There were Saturday night baths in the washtub with water heated on the stove after supper. Beginning with the baby and working up to the head of the house, we took our turns in the tub, adding some hot water for each new person.

"Of course, I should mention the little shack out back, a real necessity in those days. A potty was used in the house for training babies, then carried carefully out to be disposed of. In the middle of a cold winter night, it was not only the babies that used the potty!"

Across the country, most rural people accepted their lives of drudgery because they knew no other way. But others dreamed of a better way, perhaps having witnessed the lifestyles of their city cousins who had the benefits of electricity in their homes.

Farm families devised many different ways to keep food from spoiling, including community food lockers. Others used spring houses or lowered perishables down wells, where it was cooler.

Even small towns, including those in southeast Minnesota, had electricity. As early as 1911, Preston residents were receiving electricity from a utility built by A. H. Hanning and William Williams. A hydroelectric plant on the Root River known as the Brightsdale Plant was completed in 1915, with a line built to serve Preston, Harmony, and Canton. Service was extended to Mabel and Spring Grove in 1916, to Fountain in 1917, and to Caledonia and Houston in 1918. The Pilot Mound area had electric service beginning in 1923, when William Zimmerman built a hydroelectric facility on Trout Run to provide service to a grist mill and eighty customers through a line that became known as the "Bucksnort Line." Lanesboro also had a municipal utility served by a dam on the Root River, but the operation only provided enough power for those in the city limits.

City residents could go to bed when they pleased instead of when the light faded to dark. They could cool themselves with electric fans. They had the advantage of running water and refrigeration to keep meat from spoiling. Streetlights chased away the gloom and made it safe to walk on the streets.

Farm families looked for the light and saw it on the horizon. The lights of the city lured away the best and the brightest from the countryside. Farm families lived little better than their pioneer ancestors. Small wonder the sons and daughters of rural people saw no future on the farm and left for the cities in droves.

In the 1930s, only about 10 percent of the nation's farms had central station electric service. In Minnesota, that figure was even lower at 7 percent. This condition stood out in stark contrast to the rest of the civilized world, where 90 percent of Japanese farms, almost 95 percent of French farms, and 100 percent of Dutch farms had electricity.

The problem in the United States? Privately owned utilities could not see turning a profit on the sparsely populated rural areas. In business to make money for their stockholders, these power companies turned a blind eye to the farmers who came to them begging for electricity.

In some areas the power companies did offer to extend service, but only if the farmers would pay the high cost of building the power lines while still allowing the power companies to own them. One farmer compared this to buying a tractor but letting the dealer keep the title.

In the cases where power was extended into the countryside, rates were excessively high, ranging from eight cents a kilowatt-hour to as much as forty cents. The National Electric Light Association formed a committee to investigate rates being

Window light and smoky kerosene lanterns were the only sources of light for those without electricity. Many children suffered from poor eyesight due to the strain of doing chores with inadequate light.

charged to rural people. The committee's report showed that average rates were twelve to thirteen cents per kilowatt-hour for lights and ten cents per kilowatt-hour for farm power. In the depths of the Great Depression, farm families could not afford those rates, let alone the $2,000- to $3,000-per-mile cost of building the lines.

"The first reaction to every proposal had to be 'will it pay us?' not 'will it promote the general welfare,'" wrote Harry Slattery, who would serve as director of the Rural Electrification Administration from 1939 to 1940. "Doubtless, after

This hydroelectric dam built near Pilot Mound supplied a small amount of power to people on the Bucksnort Line. Photo courtesy of the Minnesota Historical Society.

1915 the utilities could have extended service to many hundreds of thousands of farms at a reasonable profit. But what holding company or stockbroker was interested in 6 percent on actual cash investment on farm lines, when 10 to 50 percent could be made in urban business?"

Some thought electricity would never come to rural areas. An article in *Popular Mechanics* magazine echoed that sentiment:"Thousands of these rural homes will never enjoy the blessings of electricity if they wait for the high lines to bring it because they are in areas so sparsely populated that power lines can not be made to pay for themselves."

The article encouraged farmers to generate their own power using windchargers or generators powered by gasoline, kerosene, or acetylene.

Many farmers did turn to these devices, especially the 32-volt Delco power plants. But the cantankerous machines broke down often, provided only enough power for a few lights, and were expensive to operate.

There had to be a better way. If profit was not possible, perhaps leaving that out of the equation would make the difference. In the end, it took the greatest economic disaster this country has ever faced to bring electricity to the countryside at last.

In 1929, the stock market crashed, spelling financial ruin for investors worldwide. While rural areas should have been protected from the fallout given their lack of funds to invest, the ripple effects drove the nation into deep depression. Banks failed. Businesses went under by the thousands. Checks bounced. Long lines formed outside employment agencies and families went hungry.

Meals lit only by dim lanterns or candles were not romantic affairs for American families in the days before rural electrification.

At the same time, years of drought turned the Midwest breadbasket into a dust bowl. Farms failed across the country, and Minnesota, where hordes of grasshoppers ravaged crops, was no exception. Land that had been in the same family for generations was being foreclosed on as harried farm families found it impossible to make their payments. Hard-pressed farmers needed something to make their land more productive.

The answer was electricity.

Fortunately, the country had a great leader in President Franklin D. Roosevelt. His New Deal administration set out to bring the nation back from financial ruin with a litany of lettered agencies intended to drag the nation up by its bootstraps. One of these agencies was the Rural Electrification Administration, or REA as it became affectionately known.

Roosevelt knew first-hand the plight of rural residents. Suffering from polio, the president vacationed in Warm Springs, Georgia, where the soothing waters eased the pain in his disease-stricken limbs. "There was only one discordant note in the first stay of mine at Warm Springs," Roosevelt said. "When the first-of-the-month bill came in for electric light for my little cottage, I found the charge was eighteen cents a kilowatt-hour—about four times as much as I paid in Hyde Park, New York."

President Franklin D. Roosevelt signed the executive order creating the Rural Electrification Administration on May 11, 1935. Thanks to the time he spent in Warm Springs, Georgia, FDR knew the plight of rural people who lived without electricity or were forced to pay far too much for it.

That observation started Roosevelt's study of ways to get power into rural homes at rates farmers could afford. In his message to Congress in January 1935, he set the wheels in motion toward setting up a federal agency to help build rural power lines. On May 11, 1935, he signed Executive Order No. 7037, establishing REA as an emergency agency "to initiate, administer and supervise a program of approved projects with respect to the generation of electric energy in rural areas." Relief funds were to be loaned to private power companies, municipals, and cooperatives.

A year later, REA became a permanent agency of the federal government, with $410 million to loan over ten years. Congressional leaders thought established utilities would leap at the chance to borrow low-interest money to build lines. That was not the case. When the first applications came in, not one private power company was at the table. A special committee of these for-profit utilities studied the rural situation and came up with this interesting conclusion: "There are very few farms requiring electricity for major farm purposes that are not now served."

Undaunted by the lack of interest, progressive farmers across the land decided to take matters into their own hands. Early attempts at forming electric cooperatives had shown promise. In 1919, eight non-profit farm electric cooperatives had been organized around Webster City, Iowa. Prior to the REA's start, thirty-one rural electric cooperatives had been organized in nine states.

These would be the model for REA's fledgling operations in the years following its establishment. The Rural Electrification Act of 1936 gave a clear preference for REA loans to non-profit organizations. The stage was set for farmers to start their own power companies. But could they do it? Farmers knew nothing about planning and building power lines, obtaining wholesale power, or running the business once it was established.

And not all rural people were sold on the benefits of electricity. Others, struggling with low crop and livestock prices, couldn't envision ever having the funds to pay the monthly bills, much less the five-dollar membership fee.

Undaunted, visionaries shouldered the difficult burden they knew would result in a better life for their families. Tri-County Electric Cooperative would be the result of one such effort.

Education for rural kids meant one-room schools, often lit by window light or dangerous lanterns.

Chapter 2 —
In the Beginning

The ink was barely dry on Roosevelt's executive order creating the REA when a Minnesota organization took advantage of this opportunity. On September 24, 1935, Rural Electric Service Company became the state's first REA borrower after being approved for a $100,000 loan at 3 percent interest under the Emergency Relief Appropriations Act of 1935. That group's name would later be changed to Mille Lacs Electric Cooperative.

Tri-County's turn would come one year later. But first, an all-out effort to sell the idea of an electric cooperative to the area's hard-pressed farm families would be required.

The first meeting to determine whether there was sufficient interest in the project took place on December 3, 1935, at the Lanesboro Community Hall. It was sponsored by the Lanesboro Kiwanis Club and was led by Fillmore County Extension Agent Walter Thompson. Also on the program were the Reverend S. Theo. Severtson, pastor of North Prairie Lutheran Church, and R. A. Trovatten, state commissioner of agriculture.

Trovatten, an early champion of farm electrification, told those assembled in Lanesboro, "If you really want electricity, the only thing stopping you is yourself. The money is waiting there for you. It's up to you to take the initiative. We can advise and help you, but it's your move now."

Most of the efforts to launch the rural electrification movement were led by county Extension agents, and Thompson proved up to the task. He soon organized other informational meetings, including one at the Fillmore County Courthouse in Preston held on January 15, 1936. Two weeks later, they finally acted.

Fillmore County Extension Agent Walter W. Thompson was instrumental in launching the effort that resulted in electricity for rural people. In 1935, Thompson contacted the editor of the Preston Republican *and asked for the paper's support in getting word out about the cooperative effort. After he got the ball rolling, Thompson stepped aside and let those who would benefit from its service take the helm.*

Previous page: *Posters like these from the Rural Electrification Administration kept interest in receiving power high.*

On January 30, 1936, the Fillmore County Cooperative Electric Association was formally established at a meeting presided over by temporary president Peter Abrahamson and with Thompson acting as secretary. Lynn Sheldon made the motion to form a cooperative electric association, which was promptly seconded and approved. Wilbur Heusinkveld made a motion that the cooperative be named the Fillmore County Cooperative Electric Association. That motion also passed. Then Oliver Haslerud moved the principal place of business would be Preston, Minnesota. Irving Bacon moved that the beginning of business would be February 1, 1936, and the period of incorporation would be for thirty years.

Another pioneer of the co-op's early efforts was Laurence L. Tollefson of Preston. He would be elected the first secretary/ treasurer and would become the first project superintendent.

Business continued, with Lynn Sheldon making a motion that the capital stock of the association should be $2,500. Irving Bacon moved that one share of stock be two dollars and each member be limited to one share of capital stock. Laurence Tollefson moved that the association have a limit of indebtedness of $750,000. Reverend Severtson amended that motion to $800,000. Tollefson accepted the change and the motion carried.

Heusinkveld moved that at the first annual meeting, one-third of the directors be elected for one year, one-third for two years, and one-third for three years, and at each annual meeting following the first, the directors elected hold office for a term of three years. Reverend Severtson moved that for the period preceding the annual meeting, a director from each township of Fillmore County be elected.

At the meeting, Oliver Haslerud, a Peterson farmer who was often at the forefront of any activity devoted to improving farming or the community, was elected president. Wilbur Heusinkveld of Forestville was named vice president and Laurence L. Tollefson of Preston became secretary/treasurer. Along with the officers, Elmer Tabor and Maurice Tuff would form the organization's first Executive Committee.

Oliver Haslerud was a Peterson-area farmer known to be at the forefront of every project that benefited the community. He was the co-op's first board president and would take over as project superintendent when Laurence Tollefson asked to be relieved of his duties.

The original incorporators were:

Township	Name	Address
Sumner	Will Silker	Spring Valley
Jordan	George Grieve	Chatfield
Chatfield	Frank Dudek	Chatfield
Pilot Mound	Thomas Ask	Lanesboro
Arendahl	Oliver Haslerud	Peterson
Rushford	Maurice Tuff	Rushford
Spring Valley	Elmer Tabor	Spring Valley
Fillmore	Arlo Freiheit	Wykoff
Fountain	Elvin Kline	Fountain
Carrolton	R. O. Benson	Lanesboro
Holt	John Johnsons	Whalan
Norway	Nels Byboth	Rushford
Bloomfield	Frank Hellickson	Spring Valley
Carimona	Silas Westlund	Preston
Forestville	Wilbur Heusinkveld	Spring Valley
Preston	Laurence Tollefson	Preston
Amherst	Leslie Turner	Harmony
Preble	Albert Spande	Mabel
Beaver	Ole Norgaarden	LeRoy
York	Willis Johnsons	Chester, Iowa
Harmony	Arnold Benson	Harmony
Canton	Bernard Hanson	Canton
Bristol	Earl Jones	Harmony

R. A. Trovatten, Minnesota's commissioner of agriculture, was an early champion of farm electrification who helped stir support for the project that became Tri-County Electric Cooperative. He told those assembled in Lanesboro for an early organizational meeting, "If you really want electricity, the only thing stopping you is yourself." Photo courtesy of the Minnesota Historical Society.

Before adjourning, those attending took care of some housekeeping. Board members would receive four dollars per diem for day meetings and two dollars for half-day and evening meetings, plus five cents per mile for travel to and from meetings. The secretary/treasurer received a wage of six dollars a day plus five cents per mile. Also, directors would be paid four dollars a day for surveying to determine the project's potential and selling stock.

With the job of organizing the cooperative complete, the even more challenging task of signing up members and designing the system could begin. Thompson came up with a plan that included a survey of anticipated electricity use. Executive Committee members were each assigned townships to canvas as follows:

The 1938 board of directors. Front row, left to right: Oliver Haslerud, F. B. Blanchard, and Lynn Sheldon. Back row: Guy Pierce, Nels Byboth, and George Werner. Inset: Harry Roberts.

Wilbur Heusinkveld: Bloomfield, Beaver, Forestville, York, Carimona, and Bristol
Elmer Tabor: Sumner, Jordon, Spring Valley, and Fillmore
Maurice Tuff: Rushford, Norway, Preble, and Newburg
Laurence Tollefson: Preston, Amherst, Canton, Harmony, and Holt
Oliver Haslerud: Chatfield, Pilot Mound, Arendahl, and Carrolton

The board met again in March to hear from experts including an REA field representative and E. P. Zimmerman of Minnesota Extension, who would later serve as manager of Steele-Waseca Electric Cooperative in Owatonna. Zimmerman, an electrical engineer, was charged by Extension with helping many early electric cooperatives get off the ground.

With Zimmerman's help, the board drew up plans for Project No. 1 and sent them off to REA officials in Washington, D.C. Rates also had to be set because the cost of service would be the first thing farmers asked when the directors called on them.

Will Silker suggested that the co-op offer forty kilowatt-hours per month at four dollars or one hundred kilowatt-hours at six dollars. His idea was discussed but not approved. At the next Executive Committee meeting held at Scanlon-Habberstadt Bank & Trust, rates were finally approved:

Rate A:
35 kwhs for $3.50 net
65 kwhs at 5¢ at 3.25
100 kwhs at 3¢ at 3.00
Excess at 2 ½¢ per kwh

Rate B:
100 kwhs for $5.50
150 kwhs at 3¢ at 4.50
Excess at 2¢ per kwh

But where would the wholesale power come from? That question occupied the board for the coming months. On June 2, the board met at Elmer Tabor's home to settle the power supply issue. They spent the day contacting producers of electricity to discover whether they were willing to furnish electricity to the association and to get some idea of the current rates.

The president and secretary were tasked with contacting the Olmsted County REA committee in regard to getting current for the two associations jointly. Possibilities included the municipal systems at Rochester, Lanesboro, Preston, and Spring Valley as well as Interstate Power Company and Minnesota Public Utilities.

Early crews setting the cooperative's first poles used pike poles to push them into position. This practice would continue until A-frames mounted on the backs of trucks took over the heavy lifting. From left to right are Ed Reishus, George James, and Carl Legwold.

Another interesting possibility came from residents of Granger. Board members met with game warden Art Degen and a group of people from Granger who outlined progress on a dam and lake in the vicinity. They wanted the board to look into the possibility of borrowing money from REA to construct a dam for a hydroelectric plant to supply REA projects in surrounding counties. While this idea was telegraphed to REA officials, it was not approved. The cooperative would have to find an established source for its wholesale power.

Instead, a contract with Interstate Power Company of Albert Lea was approved. This contract was to run for five years with an option for renewal.

Meanwhile, farmers in Winona County had a similar effort underway but had only signed up 150 members. At the advice of REA, the Winona County group asked to be included with Fillmore County. That was approved at the first annual meeting held November 17, 1936, at the courthouse in Preston.

On the agenda was electing a new board. It was agreed that the board would include seven directors, five from Fillmore County and two from Winona County. Voting by ballot, the following were elected: F. B. Blanchard, Lewiston; Oliver Haslerud, Peterson; Laurence Tollefson, Preston; Nels Byboth, Rushford; Harry Roberts, Harmony (on a tie-breaker with Lynn Sheldon); Guy Pierce, Utica; and Lynn Sheldon, Spring Valley. Officers were President Oliver Haslerud, Vice President F. B. Blanchard, and Secretary/Treasurer Laurence Tollefson.

To F. B. Blanchard, a veteran board member from Winona County, went the honor of throwing the switch that energized the first line.

Efforts to fine-tune the application to REA continued through the long cold winter of 1936–1937, but in the spring, a triumphant announcement came from far-off Washington: REA had approved a $167,000 allocation to build the project's first power lines! The loan was for a period of twenty years at 2.77 percent interest, with the power lines serving as security for the mortgage.

Plans were in place for 175 miles of line to serve 371 members. In REA lingo, the cooperative would forever be known as "Minnesota 32 Fillmore," signifying the state, order, and county in which it was formed.

Meeting in Preston two weeks later, the board hired Senator Henry Larson of Preston as its attorney. The Toltz, King & Day firm was hired as engineers for the project. The board also narrowly rejected a motion to join the newly organized Minnesota Rural Electric Association on a three-to-two vote.

As the project began to move forward, someone had to step up and take the reins. The board selected one of its own as project superintendent, Laurence Tollefson. He would be paid $125 a month for his services.

Ruby Nelson Shanahan recalled this period in the co-op's history in a letter she wrote that was published in the June 1985 Tri-County edition of the *Rural Minnesota News*. "I carried the first check for $22,500 down to the bank for deposit to set up the first office after Laurence Tollefson and Oliver Haslerud had secured the adequate number of easements to start the cooperative."

A crowd gathered at this substation just outside Harmony on bitter March 5, 1938, for this historic event when the first line was energized. The substation was the connecting point between the cooperative's lines and the high voltage lines from Interstate Power Company, which supplied wholesale power in the early days.

At this time, the association had sold 549 shares of stock at two dollars a share, and it had the sum of $1,098 paid into the treasury. Others, seeing the possibility of electricity on the verge of becoming reality, wanted in. The board considered a request by L. N. Hansen to contract for wholesale current for about fifty customers. He took survey blanks and planned to make a survey of his prospective customers. Blanchard and Pierce were tasked with going to Money Creek to offer them an opportunity to come in with the association.

August 12, 1937, was another landmark date for the cooperative. On this day, the board opened bids for construction of the new electric distribution system. In a sure sign that the country now was taking rural electrification seriously, eight companies submitted bids. The first choice was the Langford Electric Company, with a bid of $155,326.66. Second was Michael J. McDermott & Company, which bid $158,023.95, and third was S. J. Groves & Sons Company, with a bid of $160,133.12. At this meeting, the board appointed themselves as right-of-way men to secure a path for the line. Tollefson was excluded since he could not be both superintendent and right-of-way man.

The Langford Company, based in Minneapolis, had crews working in the area by August 25, setting poles and stringing wire. This company would become experts in rural electrification, building the first lines for cooperatives across the country. They brought with them a local man named Earl Johnson, who later would play a big role in the history of the cooperative, becoming one of its longest-serving managers.

Johnson recalled, "I grew up in Fillmore County. That's what they were looking for, a local boy. I fit that."

Johnson, who knew Oliver Haslerud, started out handling materials for the contractor. "I hauled in the first load of hardware. We were set up at Lanesboro and we started building at Harmony."

He remembers work on those early lines being slow and difficult. "This is one of the darndest parts of the country. Lots of timber to cut, and everything uphill and downhill. It wasn't like going out in the Dakotas. The truck would pull as close to the proposed line as they could and then they would pull it in with horses. The contractor had crews that would go out and dig the holes and set the poles. All that was done by hand. No mechanical equipment. At one point the contractor thought he would be smart and get a digging machine. Down here where the rock was we spent most of our time getting new gears for it. We just wore it out. We had a crew that went out and just dynamited holes. Had to use dynamite to blow the rock out. It was slow going."

The men working on the lines were some real characters, Johnson said. While the line work did not pay well and the job was backbreaking, it did provide steady income during a time when jobs were scarce.

Mr. and Mrs. Erick Rogness of rural Harmony were the first members to be hooked up to rural electrification. This picture was taken shortly after their home was energized on March 5, 1938.

"In those days there were a lot of people out of work," Johnson said. "I worked for forty cents an hour. I handled all materials to start with. I knew a guy and we rented his truck for two dollars an hour, I think. Well, he actually worked right with his truck. Some of those guys would go to work at six o'clock in the morning. They were some pretty rough guys. They liked to party and party hard. They patronized the taverns at night. They worked like a son of a gun all day and partied all night. I don't know how they did it. But they did."

With construction proceeding on schedule, Tollefson needed some help in the office he set up at the *Preston Republican*, a weekly newspaper published by Ludwig Gartner. The publisher showed a keen interest in the cooperative from its start, helping to spread the word to his readers. He also rented Tollefson space to store equipment owned by the association. Settled in the first office, Tollefson hired his first employee, Merlyn Haslerud, as stenographer and bookkeeper for fifty dollars per month.

When the second annual meeting was held on November 16, 1937, fifty-six members attended. The board authorized a five-dollar meter deposit, with 75 percent of this money being used as working capital. Westinghouse meters were ordered and 300 switches rated at 35 and 60 amps were purchased in anticipation of the current flowing.

All of this work took its toll on Tollefson, who requested to resign as superintendent in December. Oliver Haslerud would take his place.

The cooperative would get another boost that month when the Minnesota-Iowa Cooperative Light and Power Association authorized its board to transfer all of its assets to the Fillmore County group. This organization had been working hard to set up an electric cooperative in the extreme southeast part of Minnesota and the northeast corner of Iowa. But REA officials deemed them too small to succeed and encouraged the merger. This added a third Minnesota county, Houston, to the effort.

In Houston County, a Catholic priest, Monsignor A. E. Wermerskirchen of St. Peter's Church in Hokah, was chiefly responsible for getting members signed up in the same way North Prairie Lutheran Church Pastor S. Theo Severtson did in his area. The merger would add 475 new members to the growing project.

Y, MINNESOTA, THURSDAY, APRIL 7, 1938. — NUMBER 29

REA Is Now Reality

More Than Two Years of Work Bears Rich Fruit

From the Preston Republican for April 7, 1938.

This was the headline in the Preston Republican *on April 7, 1938, not long after the first lines were energized for the rural electric project. The* Republican's *editor helped make the project a reality with favorable coverage of the early efforts.*

Once again a new board was required, consisting of Oliver Haslerud, Mark Corcoran, E. F. Luehr, F. B. Blanchard, Guy Pierce, George Werner, and Nels Byboth.

The brutal Minnesota winter slowed progress, with the Langford Company asking for an extension of its January 19, 1938, deadline. The board granted an additional sixty days.

Now a new wrinkle developed. REA had long arms that often reached out from Washington to put an iron finger in a project's operations. Higher rates were ordered by the agency, much to the dismay of those working to sign on skeptical farmers. One director stated that he had interviewed more than fifty prospective members in the last two weeks, and that, in his opinion, 50 percent of them would drop out if the rates contained in said letter were adopted. REA must have acquiesced, because rates adopted by the board were more in line with what was promised to members: four dollars for the first forty kilowatt-hours, with that being the minimum, and $2.50 minimum for village residents.

On February 16, Haslerud was retained as project superintendent and manager over three other applicants. A month later, the day everyone had worked for in the past two years took place.

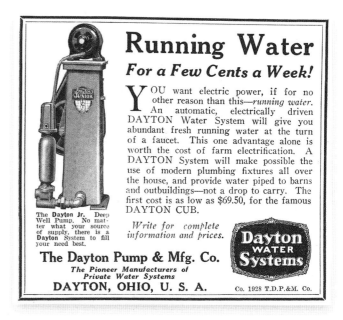

Above left: This ad was typical of the many congratulatory ads run in the Lewiston Journal by area businesses after power began to flow across the cooperative's new lines. Many businesses were quick to realize that they could profit from selling appliances to co-op members.

Above right: One of the first things electric cooperative members did after receiving electricity was to install indoor plumbing.

Snow still covered the ground on bitter March 5, 1938. Around 2 p.m., a large group gathered at the Harmony substation, where Interstate Power's transmission lines would connect with the cooperative's completed distribution system.

F. B. Blanchard, a director from Winona County, had the honor of throwing the switch that energized the first line. Inside the comfortable home of Mr. and Mrs. Erick Rogness located a half-mile southeast of Harmony, the lights came on for the first time.

"I was there for the first energization that took place over at Harmony," said Johnson, who grew up without electricity himself. "They tied in there and we fired up the first farms around there. Oh gosh, celebration! Everybody came in to see the lights. In daytime. It was a wish come true. It was almost a salvation. We had quite a gathering out at the Interstate substation south of Harmony when they hooked up the first customer. That was a nice celebration."

Area newspapers praised the achievement. The *Lewiston Journal* wrote in its March 25, 1938, edition:"In commemoration of this great event, we now give you electric light. Thus in a small and simple way, we symbolize the advent of light and distribution of electric energy, to serve in countless ways those who have subscribed for its service.

"From a small beginning two years ago, this project has continued to grow, and has now reached such proportions. By the aid of the Rural Electrification Administration and the undaunted courage and energy of those men who were active in bringing into existence the Fillmore County Cooperative Electric Association—a cooperative that now commands the respect, good wishes, and good will of the various communities it will serve—it is by this combination of forces that you now have light."

In that same edition, local businesses lined up to provide appliances to the first to have power. E. A. Wellman offered a lamp providing the "very latest in indirect lighting" for eight dollars and also touted its Hoover and Royal vacuums. Peterson & Benike Hardware offered Speed Queen wringer washers, waffle irons, toasters, and fans. Even Lewiston's Chevrolet dealer got in the act, supplying Norge refrigerators. The paper ran a story on electric fences, and told where to get them: Eustermann Brothers Farm.

Convincing prospective members to part with five dollars for a membership was no easy task. Often women—who had much to gain from electricity in the home—led the charge.

"Once we got the thing going everyone wanted electricity," Earl said. "So a lot of people went off to school and became local electricians. They tried to keep up with the wiring of the homes and farms. When I think back, you could wire a farm for $150."

Southeast Minnesota finally would have its lights! But the work was just beginning. Many challenges and triumphs would take place before those early pioneers could be satisfied with their efforts. However, any remaining skeptics only had to travel to the Harmony area to see proof that electricity was really coming.

Once electricity came to rural people, they were fascinated by what it could do for them. Here, joy fills the eyes of students as their teacher prepares to turn on the light in her class.

Chapter 3—
Tri-County Comes of Age

Success! The current was flowing, the lights were glowing. But for those involved with getting the cooperative started, there was no time to rest. They knew that many similar efforts had "died aborning." A lot of work remained to be done.

For one thing, Haslerud needed someone to keep the current flowing. Burton Saye was hired as the cooperative's first lineman. The board approved giving Haslerud authority to pay no more than ninety dollars a month but to try to hire him for seventy-five dollars per month if possible. They also authorized the purchase of any tools he might need.

A truck was bought for $600 ($200 down and $400 in ninety days) from Rushford Wagon Company, with no charge for lettering applied to the door. An application was submitted to REA for an additional $25,000 to complete the first section and bring additional members on board.

In time the best efforts of Oliver Haslerud could not meet the management needs of the growing cooperative. In 1938, the board hired Earl Kjos of Lanesboro, shown here, as its first real manager.

The hectic pace of the cooperative clearly called for someone with more experience running a business than Haslerud could offer. On April 20, 1938, a special meeting was called. At that

Previous page: *Harry Arnold is at the wheel of the cooperative's ancient pole truck/trailer.*

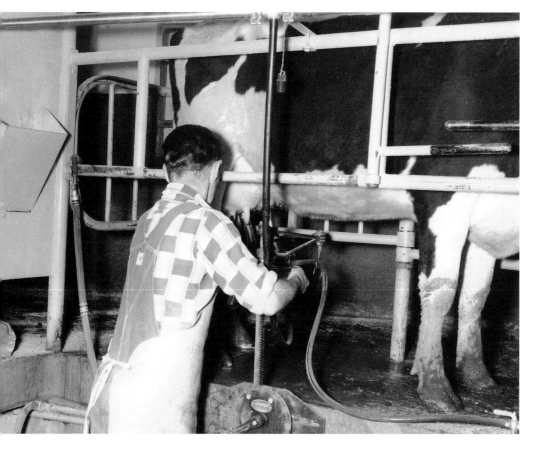

The area's dairy farmers were quick to increase herd sizes now that cows could be milked with electricity.

meeting, Earl Kjos of Lanesboro was hired as manager, with the president casting the deciding vote. A motion was passed expressing the board's appreciation for Haslerud's service during the last three years.

A second lineman, Harry Roberts, was authorized to maintain the association's line in Winona County up to the point where the three-phase line commences. He was paid one dollar per call.

In June, the first commercial account, the Hunt Haven Hotel, came on board. Two months later, REA approved a $573,000 loan that would add 520 miles of line in Fillmore, Houston, Mower, Olmsted, and Winona counties. The Langford Company, still in the area and ready to start immediately, got the nod for the new construction.

Things were progressing nicely for the cooperative. A foreman was hired at fifty cents a day to oversee clearing of right of way. Kjos and his assistant, Mrs. Haslerud, were both granted raises, and the board solved the problem of getting houses wired in advance of the line construction by approving loans to members. The low-interest loans could also be used to install indoor plumbing.

When the third annual meeting was held on November 15, 1938, there were 1,900 paid-up members. Anticipating more growth, the debt limit was raised to $2 million, an amount that no doubt stunned the audience. Line construction continued at an unflagging pace, slower than in the prairie areas but steady nonetheless.

Two new line sections would get underway in 1939, with the Langford Company again doing the work. As the miles of line expanded, a second pickup truck was purchased. Another problem was solved as REA relaxed its rules, allowing the cooperative to loan money for appliances.

Clearly the cooperative was on solid footing financially. In April 1939, the board heard from a representative of the *Minnesota Electric Farmer* and agreed to subscribe to the publication for members at the rate of one and a half cents per copy. This would begin the cooperative's practice of communicating with members through various means.

At its May meeting, the board approved adding another pickup truck and accepted the Langford Company's $274,398.09 bid for Section II. The completion date was to be November 1, 1939. Part of this line would include Houston County to the riverfront in Winona County.

Two more employees were added, Ellery Ryan as lineman and Ronald Hammock as maintenance man.

With the cooperative now about to serve in multiple counties, the name was no longer appropriate. In October 1939, the cooperative became Tri-County Electric Cooperative. The office also moved to a more central location in Rushford. Both changes had to be approved at the annual meeting in November, which prompted some controversy among the 577 members in attendence: 116 voted against the name change and 153 voted against the move to Rushford.

While elsewhere fledgling electric cooperatives struggled to make ends meet, Tri-County was growing stronger every year. In 1940, the wiring loan fund was increased to $8,000. The cooperative offered to pay members two dollars for each new member they could bring in. Regular wage increases were given to employees and three more trucks, including a one-and-a-half-ton model, were added.

Most telling was the board's action to set aside 3 percent of gross sales for an emergency maintenance fund. By the 1940 annual meeting, there were 2,200 members. A new REA loan for $185,000 was announced. It would allow service to an additional 547 members. A committee was formed to look into purchasing land for the construction of a new office building. A ten-dollar rebate toward the installation of electric ranges was offered.

Leonard "Sam" Helleland kept the early line crews on task.

Line crews often rode to the job site in the back of this "covered wagon" truck. Shown here are, from the left, Purkey Thompson, Hubert Nordness, Ben Hasleiet, Sid Arnold, Vernon James, and Forest Giesler.

By February 1941, the list of employees was as follows:

Earl Kjos

Ellery Ryan

M. F. Whitney

Ronald Hammock

Ione Harmon

Lawrence Dubbs

Lycyle Johnson

Earl Johnson would join the staff later that year as store clerk.

Just as the cooperative's effort to light the countryside had gained critical mass, a distant event would bring its efforts to a halt. On December 7, 1941, Japanese planes attacked Pearl Harbor. In short order, the United States was at war.

The cooperative quickly found itself in a strange and ironic position. Farmers nationwide were being asked to do everything possible to become more productive so the nation could feed its hungry army, yet wartime shortages of materials the cooperative required caused progress on wiring the farms to cease. The one thing farmers needed to become

Above: *James Baker, shown with a framed pole ready to be set, was the cooperative's line superintendent.*

Left: *In the early days, poles were loaded onto the trailer by hand. The poles were shipped in by rail and dumped on a siding near the depot and the M. Johnson elevator. Shown here in 1947 are Harry Arnold, George James, Jake Gutterson, and Sam Helleland.*

Linemen posed in front of their trucks for this group shot in the 1940s. The cooperative liked to hire local people as linemen because many of the men who came in with contractors could not handle working in the bitterly cold northern winters.

more productive—electricity—would be denied them because copper wire was deemed more important for planes, ships, and tanks than for rural electric power lines.

The government decreed that any project that was 40 percent complete as of December 5, 1941, could be finished. All new projects were put on hold unless they were considered essential to the war effort or considered necessary for public health. Within three months, all work on REA lines was halted regardless of their status. However, investor-owned utilities were allowed to continue work. Frustration out of this obvious double standard led to the formation of the National Rural Electric Cooperative Association (NRECA) in March 1942.

Tri-County showed its patriotism by purchasing war bonds and guaranteeing that any employee serving in the Armed Forces would have a job waiting for them upon their honorable discharge. One of these would be newcomer Earl Johnson, who served for thirty-two months in the Army. Discharged in 1945, he would return to his job in Rushford as promised.

Frustration ran high at the cooperative as members begged for line extensions across the service area. In response, the board passed this resolution directed at REA:

WHEREAS, the present emergency has made it impossible to build and complete REA lines, because of the lack of copper wire,

WHEREAS, O.P.M. has made it necessary for REA to allot materials, as well as money, and

WHEREAS, the engineering firms doing staking and engineering work are finding it impossible to hold their organizations together, and

WHEREAS, it makes a much better line to install poles before freezing weather in our Minnesota climate, and

WHEREAS, our members do not fully realize how the shortage of materials is holding up the building of the proposed extensions and

WHEREAS, it is becoming increasingly difficult to get house wiring materials, and

WHEREAS, we appreciate that the REA staff is doing all in its power to bring our members electric service as fast as it can possibly do so and

WHEREAS, it is not the intention that this resolution shall affect the priority of any allotment now on schedule;

NOW, THEREFORE, WE the undersigned state association of Minnesota do hereby petition the administrator of REA to allow the applications and loan division to make partial allotments at once on the basis of materials that are now available.

While wartime shortages forced new construction to stop, the progressive board and management of Tri-County saw other opportunities for growth. As early as February 1941, the cooperative had shown interest in purchasing the assets of the Minnesota Utilities Company. The board instructed Kjos to investigate and secure all the information he could on its value, service area, and ownership and report back to the board.

This cinderblock building served as the cooperative warehouse. Note the A-frame mounted to the back of the truck at right, used for setting poles. At this time, trucks were being modified to be of more use to the crews as they worked on lines.

On March 26, 1942, a representative of the Banister Engineering Company of St. Paul explained the details of the utility to the board. Board member George Werner met with officials of the company to negotiate its purchase. At a special meeting held on April 27, 1942, a motion to buy the company for $386,000 was approved. The transfer of assets would begin on September 30, 1942, with a deadline of December 31, 1942, for completion.

Under an agreement worked out in St. Louis, Dairyland Power Cooperative would agree to buy the system's two Root River hydroelectric generation plants. Tri-County's purchase included a distribution system serving Canton, Fountain, Houston, Prosper, and South Rushford and wholesale lines serving Caledonia, Harmony, Mabel, Peterson, and Spring Grove. Also included was a diesel generating plant in Caledonia and the right to supply wholesale power to communities already being served.

This system had an interesting history worth noting here. In 1911, A. H. Hanning and William Williams founded a power company to serve Preston. The company incorporated the following year as the Root River Power and Light Company.

A dam and a power plant known as the "Brightsdale Plant" was built on the Root River north of Lanesboro. This ingenious piece of engineering involved tunneling through solid rock at a point where a horseshoe bend in the river promised a short path from one side of the bluff to the other. When completed, water flowed through the tunnel to turn the plant's turbine. A line was built to serve Preston, Harmony, and Canton. The line was energized in 1915. Service was extended to Mabel and Spring Grove in 1916, to Fountain in 1917, and to Caledonia and Houston in 1918.

In 1929, the company was sold to the Federal Public Service Company and in 1930 another Root River hydroelectric plant was added at Rushford. In 1934, the property was sold to Minnesota Utilities Company and eventually became part of the cooperative.

The war years must have been rough ones for the cooperative employees who remained in Rushford. For the next five years, the cooperative would operate in the red.

Sid Arnold, one of four Arnold brothers to work for Tri-County, climbs a pole while Ben Hasleiet and Hubert Nordness hoist tools and hardware to him. Sid started working for the co-op in 1942, and later was killed when he came into contact with a power line. This photo was taken at the Richard Anderson farm in Pine Creek Valley.

Kjos would retire in 1946, having seen the cooperative through eight years of its formation. His replacement was Ray Domini of Lancaster, Wisconsin, who would barely last through the year. Director George Werner, who joined the board in 1937 with the Houston County merger, would step in as interim manager. In June 1948, the board would ask REA to approve making Werner's appointment as manager permanent. He would serve in that capacity until his retirement on April 5, 1961.

Werner found the cooperative prepared to make up for wartime inactivity. A warehouse tour left the board feeling confident that the warehouse was well stocked for this summer's demands. The July 27 board meeting featured a lengthy discussion on future power needs.

Paul Gunderson and Vincent Tabor from Spring Valley came before the board asking for service. They had a notice telling them to get their homes wired three years ago and felt they had waited long enough. Later a delegation from Spring Valley came to the board asking for better service on a line that was part of the Minnesota Utilities deal. There were eleven farms being served by one transformer.

Under terms of the recently passed Pace Act, the cooperative asked REA to extend the terms of its existing and future loans from twenty-five years to thirty-five years. At the time, Tri-County was serving 5,250 members with 1,865 miles of line. Estimates showed there remained about 3,250 still without service, which would require 1,100 miles of new construction. Ultimate monthly consumption was expected to be 350 kilowatt-hours per member, but it wouldn't take long before that figure was surpassed.

With 197 miles of construction under way and 101 miles of transmission rehab, and with 137 miles of line waiting to be built, more manpower and equipment became necessary. A board purchasing committee recommended increasing the size of the construction crews and adding a half-ton truck equipped with a boom, two winches, and a side sheave for rolling up wire, a one-and-a-half-ton truck for hauling construction equipment to the job site equipped with a platform and a stake body, and a Willy's pickup with a winch to be used to carry men to and from work, pull wire, and do other jobs and to eliminate bringing in the larger trucks each evening. The total investment for all of this was $11,000.

In May 1949, a new record was reached in revenue, but along with it came a new high for cost of service. "The cooperative is showing a steady growth in consumers and income," the board minutes reflected. "The manager says that at present pace and average luck by December 1, 1949, all applicants for electric service who had waited over one year will have service."

Occasionally, a line was built to serve people in poor health. One was for Albert Lang. According to the minutes: "Mr. Lang's is a case where we feel that on account of condition of health of both Mr. and Mrs. Lang we are justified

In building to them, also Kenneth Ness. At request of the Fillmore County nurse, we authorize the manager to provide electric service to Frank Eick of Wykoff who is a cripple from arthritis, as a gesture of sympathy for his affliction." Special arrangements also were made to serve the Parochial Evangelical Lutheran School at Silo, near the village of Lewiston.

With the finances in excellent shape, and transmission construction nearly 100 percent, the cooperative increased the number of employees to sixty-six and also enlarged the door on the garage to allow larger trucks to enter. Apparently this was prompted by several mishaps involving equipment that was not properly stowed!

Electric milk coolers meant less spoiled milk and more profit for dairy farmers.

As the 1940s drew to a close, the manager's report showed more income and more expenses—and also revealed that "there are now some homes heated by electricity, all of which makes us stop and think what the demand may be and whether or not we can meet it. Some farmers are installing unusual equipment that is overloading the transformers."

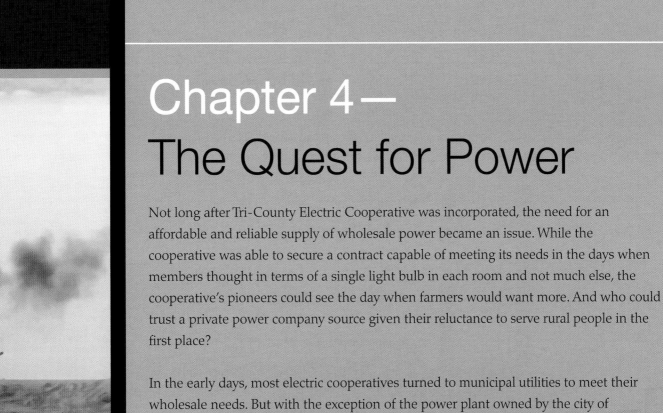

Chapter 4 —
The Quest for Power

Not long after Tri-County Electric Cooperative was incorporated, the need for an affordable and reliable supply of wholesale power became an issue. While the cooperative was able to secure a contract capable of meeting its needs in the days when members thought in terms of a single light bulb in each room and not much else, the cooperative's pioneers could see the day when farmers would want more. And who could trust a private power company source given their reluctance to serve rural people in the first place?

In the early days, most electric cooperatives turned to municipal utilities to meet their wholesale needs. But with the exception of the power plant owned by the city of Rochester, few municipal utilities in the area had the extra capacity to supply a decent-sized electric cooperative once things got going. Because the city's native load had to come first, electric cooperatives dependent on municipal power sources saw their members cut off during periods of heavy use.

Imagine heading out to the barn to milk the cows using your new electric milkers. You doubled the herd size because of how much more efficient the electric milkers made your operation. But just when you need electricity the most, the power is cut off. Farmers across Minnesota faced this dilemma as early as the late 1940s.

This forced many of Minnesota's electric cooperatives to negotiate contracts with often hostile private power companies, which had no incentive to see its rivals succeed.

Previous page: *When word that Wisconsin's electric cooperatives were considering joining forces to supply their own wholesale power, Tri-County was interested in joining the project. Tri-State Cooperative began work on its first plant located in Genoa, Wisconsin, in 1940. The Genoa Station project began supplying power from its two 3,000-kilowatt generating units a year later.*

With the completion of Alma Station in 1947, Dairyland Power was finally able to meet the entire power needs of its member systems. It would be Dairyland's largest power plant until 1969, when the giant Genoa G-3 plant came on line.

There is no indication that Tri-County, which partnered with Interstate Power Company for its wholesale needs, ever faced these critical shortages. But it is apparent that the board sensed trouble was coming at an early date and took immediate steps to make sure this problem never plagued its members.

When talk of a cooperative-owned power plant located in Wisconsin crossed the Mississippi River, Tri-County's board was immediately interested. This would be a new breed of cooperative, one that did not provide electricity to end users but instead to a group of cooperatives. At its February 23, 1939, regular meeting held at the First State Bank in Rushford, the board took up the idea of getting involved with this project.

The bylaws and articles of incorporation for what was then called the Tri-State Power Cooperative were read and a free and open discussion was entered into as to its merits and demerits. On a motion by Haslerud, and seconded by Corcoran, the co-op elected three delegates to attend a meeting in March 1939 to be held at Prairie du Chien, Wisconsin, on the subject of a proposed generating plant at Genoa, Wisconsin. The motion carried. A second motion by the same two directors called for Tri-County to cooperate with the new power cooperative.

A motion was then made by Leuhr and seconded by Haslerud that the secretary/treasurer be authorized to buy three memberships in Tri-State Power Cooperative. Nels Byboth, Mark Corcoran, and F. B. Blanchard would represent Fillmore County.

While most of the nation's electric cooperatives would not tackle the critical power supply problem until years later, Tri-County and other cooperatives in the north-central region were off to an early start. Their forward thinking would pay huge dividends in the coming years and would serve as a model that electric cooperatives across the country would follow.

Starting with the ill-fated proposal to build a hydroelectric power plant in Fillmore County, Tri-County's board showed its interest in being energy self-sufficient. They found like-minded individuals

This is Dairyland's Genoa 1 station shown from the top of the nearby bluff. The plant was completed in 1941. When it came on line, it was the largest cooperative power plant and the first to transmit power across state lines. Most of the power cooperative's plants were located on the Mississippi River to provide easy access to coal barges.

Mired in unexpected controversy, the Flambeau Hydro Station, shown here under construction in 1949, became a symbol of the cooperatives' political and electrical power. It was finally completed in 1951.

In 1962, the Atomic Energy Commission signed a contract with Dairyland to build an $18-million nuclear reactor to power a 50,000-kilowatt generator at its Genoa site. The unit was an experimental design the commission wanted to perfect for export to developing nations. Delays in the design and construction of the LaCrosse Boiling Water Reactor postponed operation until 1967, when it became the first electric cooperative-owned nuclear power plant.

across the great river in Wisconsin. The germ of the power cooperative idea came in 1937 when Arthur Hitt, a state representative and pioneer of the Buffalo Electric Cooperative, petitioned REA to fund construction of a cooperative generating plant in his region.

"I doubt whether we could go through another winter without energy and keep our members in line," he wrote. "…I am afraid that the Northern States Power Company will make inroads on our membership."

Joined by Clark County Extension Agent Wallace Landry and dozens of other rural electric cooperative leaders in central Wisconsin, Hitt's pleas were heard by the REA field man, George Lewis, who was working in the area. "We have in this splendid dairy section a class of customers that will not stop at an average use of 100 kilowatt-hours per month. I will be surprised if we do not see an average annual consumption of around 2,000 kilowatt-hours."

Those searching for a new source of power found a kindred spirit in REA engineer Franklin P. Wood. An unabashed technocrat, Wood believed society's problems could be solved by investment in new technology and increased efficiency to pull the people up by their bootstraps. The REA program proved fertile ground for his ideals.

Wood succeeded in convincing his superiors at REA to let him build a cooperatively owned power plant centered around the 9,000 members served by eight electric cooperatives located around Eau Claire, Wisconsin. His plan included forming a new cooperative owned by the eight distribution systems. In this manner, electric cooperatives would not only control the distribution of power to members but also the generation and transmission roles.

This generation and transmission cooperative, or G&T, was named the Wisconsin Power Cooperative. Organizers applied for a $150,000 REA loan and set a ceiling of $2.5 million to meet its construction needs. In March 1938, the first electric cooperative-owned power plant in the United States began sending power to rural people in western Wisconsin.

The 2,100-kilowatt Chippewa Diesel Station as it was called was tiny in comparison to the mighty precedent it set. Here was an example every cooperative in the nation could follow and soon did. Finally, rural people shunned by the private power companies could control their own destiny.

A year later, interest in the project from cooperatives in Iowa and Minnesota—along with five other systems in Wisconsin that could not get loans until a power source was found—prompted Wood to suggest dramatically expanding the power

All the power generated by Dairyland would be of no use if it were not for the network of transmission lines that carry it to member systems in three states. Engineering and construction methods originally designed by Dairyland engineers have become the standard for transmission lines throughout the world.

Linemen working for Dairyland knew no fear of heights as they scaled the giant poles set atop equally giant bluffs near the Mississippi River.

cooperative concept. He proposed forming the Tri-State Cooperative and asking REA to fund a feasibility study to better serve cooperatives in a three-state region.

By the end of the year, REA approved a $500,000 loan to build a coal-fired steam plant located in Genoa, Wisconsin, that would be three times the size of the Chippewa Falls plant. Before the project could start, a tempting offer from a private power company was dangled in front of the electric cooperative leaders, but the offer was soundly rejected. Construction of the two 3,000-kilowatt generating units began in May 1940 and the project began supplying electricity a year later.

The Genoa plant was the largest built by an electric cooperative at the time and the first to send electricity across state lines. Solidly in the fold was Tri-County Electric Cooperative, along with neighboring Freeborn-Mower Electric Cooperative, three electric cooperatives in northeast Iowa, and Wisconsin cooperatives located as far south as the Illinois state line.

With power flowing from the plant, talk of a tie line north to the Wisconsin Power Cooperative power plant began in earnest. The two power cooperatives had the same mission of serving rural people with plentiful power, and the Tri-State plant was built with the future in mind and had plenty of excess power to share with its neighbor. In the summer of 1941, plans began for two 4,000-kilowatt generators at its Genoa station.

Wisconsin Power, on the other hand, was having trouble meeting its members' needs. At least once in the summer of 1941 it had to cut off power to a member system.

It was inevitable that the two systems would join forces. That historic event took place just days after the bombing of Pearl Harbor, when representatives of both systems approved the deal and Dairyland Power was formed. In the words of cooperative attorney Floyd Wheeler, "On the morning of December 16, 1941, Dairyland Power did not exist. By midnight of that day, a power cooperative with millions in assets and serving thousands of people had been created."

Constant upgrades and improvements to the transmission system have kept Dairyland's wholesale power supply ahead of the growth of its member systems.

This consolidation did not signal the end of power supply problems for Dairyland and its member systems. The United States' entry into World War II brought critical shortages of supplies for member systems. It also caused headaches for Dairyland. The two units destined for the Genoa station were instead requisitioned by the Navy, where they reportedly were carted off to Puerto Rico and left to rust without generating a single watt.

At this time, the far-sighted Dairyland directors, seeing the increased demand for electricity when the war would end, commissioned an engineering study that showed serious flaws in the system. The study showed that the 49,345 members under the Dairyland umbrella required 29,000 kilowatts of power; however, Dairyland could only deliver 23,200 kilowatts.

In response, Dairyland entered a tremendous building phase, adding a 40,000-kilowatt coal-fired power plant at Alma, a 5,000-watt diesel plant at Baldwin, and began the tedious political battle of building a hydroelectric plant on the Flambeau River. That project would not begin generating until 1951.

Dairyland's massive G-3 power plant used a high pressure, double-steam reheat system to generate more than half of Dairyland's power needs the first year it was part of the system. It can generate 350,000 kilowatts of power.

In 1962, Dairyland signed a contract with the Atomic Energy Commission to build an experimental nuclear reactor to create steam for a 50,000-kilowatt generator. Though small, this unit would open the door, it was hoped, to a much larger nuclear power plant with promises of delivering power that was "too cheap to meter." When the plant opened in 1967, it was the first cooperative-owned nuclear plant in the nation. However, plans for another nuclear power plant were scrapped in 1979.

Dairyland would build at least one power plant before the end of each decade of its existence to meet the growing demand for electricity.

As the years passed by, Dairyland's member systems continued to add members and load. The G&T now serves twenty-five electric cooperatives with more than 250,000 members who use an average of 1,144 kilowatt-hours per month, far more than the 1941 prediction of 2,000 kilowatt-hours a year. It also supplies wholesale power to sixteen municipal systems. The miles of transmission line built, sometimes in precarious conditions, was impressive. Starting with 350 miles of 69-kilovolt line and 160 miles of 34.5-kilovolt line in 1948, Dairyland today has more than 3,100 miles of line.

Stories abound of the rough-and-tumble men who built these lines. On Monday mornings, supervisors knew to look in the county lock-ups for any missing crew members. One story tells of the linemen who winched their Army surplus truck up a bluff so steep that the truck ended up dangling from the winch line. Fortunately, strict safety standards today mean crews no longer take these kinds of risks.

Dairyland Power Cooperative now owns and operates eleven power plants that can generate 1,261 megawatts of power. Its baseload coal-fired power plants are located along the Mississippi River in Wisconsin, allowing easy access to barges delivering fuel. It also has natural gas, hydroelectric, landfill gas, and animal waste-to-energy power plants in Wisconsin. Dairyland purchases wind and additional landfill gas generation from renewable energy facilities in Wisconsin, Minnesota, and Iowa.

Environmental regulations have added millions to the cost of generating electricity, including the baghouse and scrubber added to the G-3 plant. Concerns over the release of carbon dioxide from power plants created huge uncertainty in the industry as this book was completed.

It has 611 employees, 277 substations, and $1.2 billion in assets, making it one of the largest cooperative-owned G&Ts in the nation.

While Dairyland faces many challenges in meeting the power supply needs of Tri-County Electric Cooperative and its other member systems, it continues its mission of supplying all the power needed at the lowest possible cost. The success of Tri-County Electric Cooperative would not have been possible without the companion success of Dairyland. Over the years, Tri-County would learn it could rely on its "big brother" for much more than power supply.

"I think it has been a good partnership," said Brian Krambeer, president and CEO of Tri-County Electric. "From the uncertainty in the industry, it's pretty obvious being able to control your destiny and work together with all twenty-five member distribution systems has certainly been a good thing. It gets back to risk management. If we are all by ourselves, we are a little vulnerable. But by working together and committing our resources, we are stronger. I think that relationship has been very positive."

In the words of Wisconsin Power Cooperative organizer and long-time Dairyland president John Olson, "There is a destiny that makes us brothers. We cannot go this way alone. What we put back into the lives of others, comes right back into our own."

Chapter 5—
The Dream Becomes Reality

Despite setbacks from the Korean War, which again siphoned off manpower and materials, Tri-County's employees worked hard to get the dream of area coverage realized. In fact, Manager Werner was working so hard that the board passed a resolution at its December 1951 meeting telling him to either take a month of vacation with pay or be dismissed for a month without pay.

Tri-County Electric was deeply involved at the time with helping the Fillmore County Telephone Cooperative get off the ground. Werner took over managing the phone co-op as well, and he made several trips to REA offices in Washington, D.C., on its behalf.

With the power supply issue solved, and all the new construction in high gear, more room at the headquarters was required for the sixty-six employees. The February 1950 board minutes reflect these concerns: "It is becoming more and more apparent that our office space is inadequate for maximum

This was home to Tri-County Electric Cooperative from 1951 until a new building was constructed in 1982.

efficiency. The cooperative owns a 50 x 50 foot lot at the rear of the present office building which could be used to advantage." After much discussion (then, as now, building new office space is not done lightly), the board set up a committee to study the building situation.

Previous page: *Manager George Werner, left, shakes hands with car dealer Vince Miller after the co-op took delivery on several new trucks in 1948. Behind the salesman are Line Superintendent Milton Poepel and board member Ed Leer.*

In 1950, a $72,000 loan from REA would finance the remodeling of the office building, extending it onto a lot created when the co-op purchased and demolished the nearby Byboth Heating Company. The board also agreed to purchase the Eggen garage, which was used to store equipment. The sale included a Model T truck, which was used for a time to haul trash and later disposed of in 1950.

In its application to REA for remodeling funds, the board stated that the heating system "is such to hamper efficient work and is the cause of some physical distress to employees." In 1951, the cooperative moved into new quarters, where it would remain until 1981.

Women, ever the driving force behind rural electrification because it freed them from the drudgery of housework, learned to "live better electrically" from this display in Tri-County's office lobby.

At the same time, the cooperative purchased its first mechanical hole-digger. "They laid off a bunch of people when they bought that hydraulic digger," lineman Freddie Arnold recalled. "We had quite a few older guys digging holes and setting poles and stuff. They were good workers. Some of these guys would dig sixteen holes a day if it was decent digging."

Freddie, one of four Arnold brothers who worked for the cooperative, got his start driving trucks loaded with poles. "I used to go to the Twin Cities sometimes every week, sometimes every other week, and get a load of poles," Freddie said. "They were mostly cedar back then. I'd probably get around forty poles on. One time, I had to get some sixty-footers and a few fifties. I put the big ones on the bottom and put the smaller poles on top. I thought this would even up real good. But when I started for home I'd go over a little bump on the highway and the driver wheels would come off the ground and spin and then take off again. But I made it home okay."

Hauling, loading, and unloading poles in the days before digger/derrick trucks was a difficult and perhaps dangerous task, made even more precarious by the poor brakes on the old semi truck assigned to the job. "There were two of us," Freddie said. "I drove the truck. First we loaded, had to load by hand. It wasn't good, I'll tell ya. When I got several poles ahead a crew would come behind and put hardware on, and another crew came behind, dug, and set the poles. And then we had a wire-stringing crew. I had to help the guys with hardware. I liked that, I really did."

Getting the poles unloaded required a heavy log chain and an iron bar—and a helper with nerves of steel. "We had to figure out what pole they needed. Then we put the chain on it and we would jab the bar in the ground. He would hang back on the bar and I would drive the truck off. Sometimes it didn't work and he got madder than hell because he'd fall down," Freddie said.

"Now they use the boom for everything. Back then we had what they called a pole jack. You could get that under the pole and then come down with the handle and you could hardware the pole. We used a lot of homemade stuff, too."

The steep hills in Tri-County's service area have always made line work difficult.

The hills in the cooperative's service area are made of limestone, which made it hard to set poles. "Sometimes the engineers staking line would come to solid rock and they would put a stake there and pile rock around to hold it and they would write 'ha ha,'" Freddie said.

To get poles in the ground, Tri-County line crews learned to work with dynamite, a task they still do themselves. Freddie Arnold soon moved from hauling poles to setting them and then climbing them as well.

"This one time I remember setting poles by hand over by Mabel. Quite a bit of rock over that way. You had a back pocket full of dynamite, a cord, an eight-foot bar, a shovel, and your dinner bucket and the foreman said, 'I'll see you at quitting time.' When you got four guys digging you had to go a long way to get another hole you could dig."

He said crews often used draft horses to snake poles into areas too remote for the trucks to drive.

Utilities didn't start working from bucket trucks until the early '60s, and Tri-County would make the change much later. "I had one," Freddie said. "The superintendent bought another used one, kind of a cheap thing. Then we had two, one at Caledonia and one at Lewiston. The one at Caledonia, they got it up and couldn't get the boom down.

I had all the literature on it and I knew what we had to do. I opened up a valve and got soaked with oil. I had just got a brand new jacket. I think I threw the thing away.

"Bucket trucks, they were pretty nice, but we didn't get a chance to use it too much. Most of the line crew didn't use them, the service people got the buckets."

In those days, the linemen learned on the job instead of in carefully structured classes. Freddie witnessed his share of accidents and some fatalities, including his brother, Sid, who started working for the co-op in 1942.

Decisions carefully made in the co-op's boardroom often turned out to be the correct ones, keeping Tri-County strong for its first seventy-five years. The cooperative way of doing business means members always have a say in these decisions through their elected directors.

"I started working around Spring Valley with a guy named Clayton Roelofs," Freddie said. "He was at the co-op before I started (1944)." He worked at Harmony, had a wife and one little kid, another on the way. We were converting single-phase to three-phase. He got up there and got this arm over the hot phase. Burned off both arms up here, didn't have any elbows. I had to help get him down off the pole. I was working a couple of poles down. He's alive yet today. They made him a dispatcher. He was dispatcher a long time."

The board agreed to pay the expenses of Ronald Blake Johnson, who worked with the injured lineman and helped rescue him, and his wife to attend the Minnesota State Safety Council meeting in Duluth to receive the council's Honor Deed Citation for his work in saving the life of Clayton Roelofs. Clayton's accident happened on October 3, 1951.

Freddie and Sid were part of a crew that was working an outage on a cold day in 1959. They were changing a transformer with the line still energized to keep power on for the others on the line. "He started up the pole and another lineman started up underneath," Freddie said. "I was parked across the road getting stuff out. I heard this awful noise. He went up higher because the other guy was underneath, I guess. He slipped and I guess he grabbed that high bushing. He wasn't belted off yet.

Freddie remembered another serious injury. Bob Spartz and Arnold Peterson were working to change out an OCR on top of a pole. They were working to remove the bypass jumper when the wire fell out of Peterson's hot stick and hit Spartz in the shoulder. The shock caused him to flip upside down with his pole strap caught on Peterson's feet. Peterson teamed up with Al Froiland, who was working on the ground, to lower the injured worker using a rope. They loaded him into a service truck and took him to the hospital in Rochester. Despite injuries to one knee and shoulder, he remained with the cooperative for many more years.

"We had another one over by Spring Grove," Freddie said. "Royal Rollins, he was an older fellow, worked with a two-man crew out of Mabel. They were working at a night club and had the truck parked by the transformer pole. The other guy went up on the take-off pole to open up the line. This fellow disconnected the lightning arrestors on the transformers. He belted off. He stood on the arms and waited for him to energize the lines, you could hear it on the truck.

"I went over after it happened. Looked to me like he didn't have rubber gloves on. He reached over and grabbed the jumper coming down. That's the way things happen, you know. He was belted off, he was in good shape. He lived about a week. That was kind of high voltage, 14,400 volts."

In the late '70s, John DeGeorge also made contact while working with construction crews. He continues to work for the cooperative in the area of energy management.

Conditions for the linemen often were brutal, especially in the heart of winter, when the mercury could dip to 40 degrees below zero. Linemen only got paid when they went out to work, so they tried to find something to do even on the coldest days. Often this meant clearing brush and burning it to stay warm.

Still, the ice storms that plague many Midwestern electric cooperatives were not much of a problem for Tri-County, perhaps because of the

The annual family picnic was always a highlight for employees of the cooperative. This one was held in October 1957.

Bob Burns was hired as power use advisor to encourage members to make the most of their new "hired hand," electricity.

This 1950s vintage Chevrolet Suburban was used by the Engineering Department and also to haul people to meetings and job sites.

Meter technician Joe Rislow shows how he tests meters to two people touring the cooperative. Tri-County saved money by doing its own work whenever possible.

shelter of the river valleys. "I think the hilly country down here saved us," said Earl Johnson. "The ones out west like around Albert Lea area and even Rochester, they had more trouble with ice than we had. So we always said the hills were good for something."

"A lot of them had ice but we were lucky," Freddie Arnold said. "They had a lot more of them down south in Iowa and we had to go help them. Sometimes the ice was that big on the wires," he added, forming his hands into a circle the size of a soda can.

Tornadoes, however, were a different story. One early storm in 1950 started at Spring Valley and worked its way across the cooperative's service area, leaving devastation in its wake before it disappeared at Houston. The tornado struck a mink farm and scattered the hapless animals all over the hillside.

Tri-County crews built new lines well into the 1960s. Then, as the hard work of power use man Bob Burns paid off, the crews switched to revamping the lines to allow more current to flow. Burns was hired to show members how to take full advantage of the power of electricity. Electric cooperatives quickly learned that if they were going to stay in business, they needed members to use more than a single light bulb in each room.

"Wiring loans provided funds so members could wire homes and farms," said Earl Johnson. "We loaned money for appliances, too. We used to display stuff in our office. We put in a first-class kitchen with all the cupboards. It was kind of a demonstration thing where women could hold their meetings there and serve food."

Electric ranges became commonplace, as did vacuums, irons, washers and dryers, refrigerators, deep freezers, stock tank heaters, grain dryers, and all kinds of dairy equipment. Soon all-electric houses were being built, and the cooperatives that served them granted special all-electric rates.

"For many years we had a special rate," recalled Earl Johnson of the all-electric homes. "It got down as low as a cent and a half per kilowatt-hour. Which, it started out at ten cents, so you can see there was some efficiency in the cooperative."

Besides building lines down to the letter U (early lines were designated by letter), the cooperative also purchased the colorfully named "Bucksnort" line located in Pilot Mound Township in Fillmore County. This line served farmers in the North Prairie area and along Highway 30 from a small hydroelectric dam. "Everybody kind of envied them for a little while," Earl said. "They had electric lights way back there."

"The guy operating it, he had about 150 consumers," Freddie Arnold said. "He ran short of power. He had the dam there and the generator and that was it. Then he had to buy current from Tri-County. He wasn't getting enough current. Tri-County finally bought it and we redone the whole thing. Wish I had saved the old cutouts. They used to fuse them with an old piece of wire. The poles were short, too."

The short poles were especially hazardous given the previous owner's practice of putting the hot wire on the bottom under the assumption that it made the line less likely to be struck by lightning.

In 1953, the cooperative moved its emphasis away from construction and instead put the focus on operations and line upgrades. Its financial condition remained sound, allowing it to make advance payments on its REA loans. After making its seventh advance payment to REA in the amount of $50,000 on the B note, the board passed a resolution honoring Manager Werner:

"We, the board of directors, do herby recognize Mr. George J. Werner as an outstanding, capable and efficient manager of the Tri-County Electric Cooperative. We believe this is indicated by the fact that the cooperative has made advance payments to the United States Treasury to amount to $350,000."

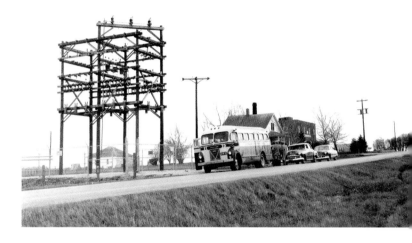

Tri-County often played host to groups wanting to learn more about the rural electrification story. This one in the early 1950s stopped at the Fremont switching station.

Tri-County's insurance company sent a representative to the co-op office to honor Herman Anderson (holding a hard hat) with its "Green Turtle Award" for wearing the proper safety gear during an incident that could have otherwise been fatal to him. Anderson, who worked on one of the maintenance crews, was hit on the head by a falling tree branch. The impact cracked his hard hat but did not seriously injure him. Also shown in this photo are Hap Clayton, left, a safety instructor from the Minnesota statewide association, and Tri-County's line superintendent, Milton Poepel, right.

Chapter 6— Electricity For All

Tri-County Electric entered a golden period in its history during the 1960s. The decade began with the cooperative joining more than 1,000 others across the nation in celebrating the twenty-fifth anniversary of the rural electrification program. Tri-County marked the event by signing on to a national advertising program called "Tell the Nation the Truth," designed to counter continuing anti-co-op propaganda from the private utilities.

During this era, the cooperative saw the dream of area coverage—in which all people in the service area had access to electricity— finally realized. No longer would rural people in southeast

Earl Johnson helped build some of the first lines for Tri-County as an employee of the Langford Construction Company. He moved to the cooperative in 1941, and became manager in 1961, a position he would hold until his retirement in 1982.

Previous page: *Shown here are the employees who worked to set the poles by helicopter in July 1982. From left to right are the co-pilot, Arless Markegard, Freddie Arnold, the chopper pilot, Rocky Carlson, and Darrell Erickson. Tri-County also used a helicopter to upgrade a line to a fishing float in the 1970s. The float, a barge located in the Mississippi, is actually in Wisconsin. Serving it demonstrated Tri-County's commitment to area coverage, the concept that anyone wanting service would get it.*

Tri-County Board President Harvey Rislow gets ready to cut the ribbon during the grand opening of the co-op's new office building as the rest of the board looks on. At left, with his hand on the ribbon, is retiring manager Earl Johnson. Behind him is his replacement, Bruce Meistad.

Minnesota be denied service or be forced to pay considerably more for what people in the cities took for granted.

When Tri-County reached its own twenty-fifth anniversary in January 1961, 95 percent of American farms had electricity while the amount was even higher in Minnesota—98.5 percent. At this time the cooperative had reached 8,000 members who were served by more than 2,700 miles of line.

Not only was electricity available, but the price was also affordable enough that most members did not worry much about their electric bill. In fact, that same month the cooperative announced a 10-percent decrease for farm, residential, and commercial rates. Members now looked for new ways to use this new servant on the farm and in the home. And with wholesale power supply in the capable hands of Dairyland Power, Tri-County's members did not have to worry about using too much power. Their only worries were about overloading the transformers and lines.

The nation stood on the threshold of an era of limitless electricity so abundant that meters would soon be obsolete, or so the prevailing wisdom said. As delusional as those times seem today, there was every reason for optimism. Electricity from nuclear power and from hydroelectric dams under construction offered a seemingly limitless supply of cheap power.

The first all-electric homes came into being in the early 1960s. Many carried a marker on their doors signifying the home as a Gold Medallion, All-Electric Home. How strange it must have seemed to the older generation to see homes being built with no chimneys.

Freddie Arnold, left, and Arnold Peterson paused in their efforts to rebuild a section of line along Highway 61 for this photo. Behind them is the Mississippi River, the co-op's eastern boundary.

Because of the difficult terrain, Tri-County's line crews resorted to extreme measures to set poles. Helicopters were used on more than one occasion to set poles that were inaccessible by vehicles. This photo shows a helicopter owned by Imperial International of St. Paul hoisting one of seven poles used to rebuild a section of line along Highway 61. It took the crew thirty-six minutes to set the seven poles.

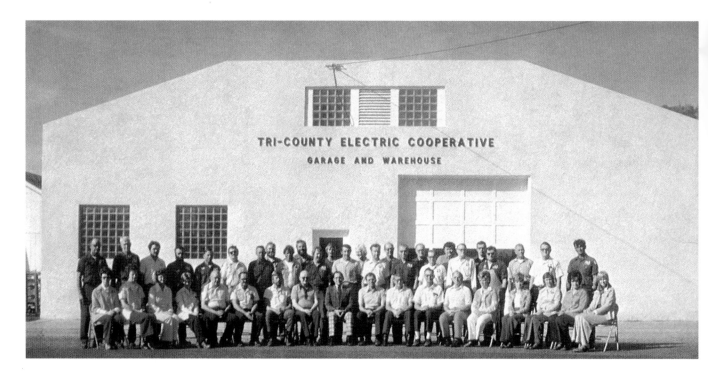

TRI-COUNTY ELECTRIC COOPERATIVE
GARAGE AND WAREHOUSE

During the 1976 bicentennial, employees of Tri-County posed for this group shot in front of the garage and warehouse.

To earn a gold medallion—considered the apex of modern living—a home had to have an electric clothes washer and dryer, waste disposal, refrigerator, and all-electric heating, often accomplished by radiant resistance cables installed in the ceiling.

The Medallion Homes campaign was a huge success. By some estimates, the nationwide goal of about 1 million all-electric homes was achieved, according to the Edison Electric Institute, although data on the actual number built is unavailable.

To keep demand for electricity high, the industry launched the Live Better Electrically campaign. It was supported nationwide by 300 electric utilities and 180 electrical manufacturers. The campaign got then-actor Ronald Reagan, the popular host of *General Electric Theater*, to take his TV audience on a series of tours of his all-electric home.

An in-house GE sales pitch declared that "there should not be a man, woman or child in America who doesn't know that you can 'Live Better Electrically' with General Electric appliances and television."

Tri-County would need a new leader to take it into this era of modern living. When long-time manager George Werner announced his retirement at sixty-eight due to "ill health and advancing years," as the co-op's newsletter related, the board would receive a huge number of applications for the job, but narrowed it down to three before

Members of the cooperative's board in 1976 are shown here with Manager Earl Johnson. They are, seated from the left: John Papenfuss of Dakota, Harvey Rislow of Lewiston, and George Mathis of Winona; standing from the left: Erling Burtness of Caledonia, Elton Redalen of Fountain, Edward Albrecht of LaCrescent, Lloyd McKenzie of Spring Valley, and Earl Johnson of Rushford.

picking the local man for the job. In the end, the board would pick office manager Earl Johnson as Werner's replacement. Except for the time he spent in the service during World War II and nine months when he tried his hand at running a hardware store, Johnson would spend his entire career at Tri-County. He would lead the cooperative through good times and bad in a storied career that continued until 1982.

Earl, who died in 2010 not long after being interviewed for this book, was known as a frugal manager who insisted the employees make the most of the members' money. "Earl was a wonderful manager," said Freddie Arnold. "He was tight; you would think it was his own money."

"Earl was not tight-fisted, but he was just a very conservative individual," recalled Bob Spartz, Tri-County's vice president of system operations. "I remember our service truck was up for replacement. We had our choice—a small V-8 motor or four-wheel drive. Not both. So we took the six-cylinder with four-wheel drive. Earl was just a conservative individual. I don't think he wanted to see the co-op in debt. It was quite a few years before we started getting a changeover in equipment."

Part of that changeover would be the cooperative's first bucket trucks, Spartz said, which arrived about the time he started working for Tri-County in the late 1960s. Other cooperatives had bucket trucks as early as 1960. Instead, Tri-County crews climbed poles or worked off a bucket attached to one of the digger derrick trucks.

"We didn't have bucket trucks," Spartz said. "The first and only one we had was a thirty-two-foot Pelican, I can remember that. That was the only bucket we had other than you could pin a bucket on the end of a digger derrick. You couldn't control it. A guy would sit in the operator's seat and run you up and down.

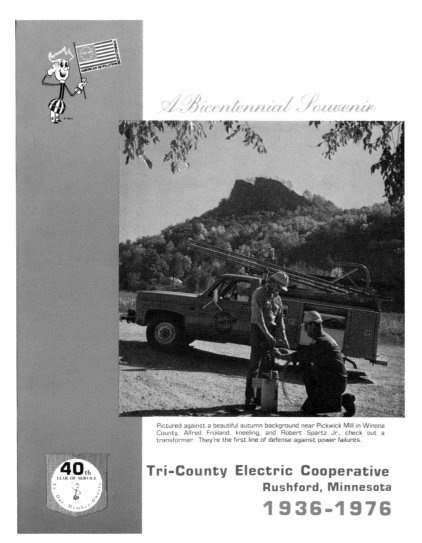

A Bicentennial Souvenir

Pictured against a beautiful autumn background near Pickwick Mill in Winona County, Alfred Froiland, kneeling, and Robert Spartz Jr., check out a transformer. They're the first line of defense against power failures.

Tri-County Electric Cooperative
Rushford, Minnesota
1936-1976

40th YEAR OF SERVICE To Our Member-Owners

"We had an old A-frame for setting poles. I was working maintenance out of Rushford here. There were four of us and we would take that A-frame and do service revamps and we dug all the holes by hand, set the poles with the A-frame. You did it the old-fashioned way compared to now."

Part of the reason bucket trucks were so slow coming to the cooperative was the difficult terrain, which often made it impossible to get trucks close enough to work on lines. So men continued to climb poles with belts and hooks.

Spartz came to work at Tri-County as an apprentice. "They put me up in the old Northwestern Hotel in downtown Rushford, it's not there anymore. It was a classic. I stayed there for a month and I ate at a restaurant across the street. That lady packed my lunch. I never got a wage, just room and board. On-the-job training, that's what it was."

Posing for the 1976 annual meeting booklet cover were Alfred Froiland and a young Bob Spartz. The photo was shot in front of the Pickwick Mill in Winona County.

If the 1960s were years of optimism and low rates, the 1970s turned that upside down. The decade featured two energy crises, the first in 1973, caused when Arab oil-producing nations put an embargo on oil in retaliation for U.S. support of Israel in the Yom Kippur War. The second came in 1979 in the wake of the Iranian Revolution. For the first time, Americans had to deal with shortages of energy, particularly gas for transportation. The call to "Electrify: Conserve Fuels in Short Supply" went out to consumers across the nation. President Nixon asked Americans to curtail their use of Christmas lights. Later, President Carter would don a sweater while asking Americans to lower their thermostats in the winter.

Tri-County's office workers tried to set a good example and follow the president's advice. "We sat with our coats on," said Lorraine Benson, director of customer service. "The windows frosted up, it was so cold in the winter. We did our part, that's for sure. I can even remember the coat I wore. It was really long because I was wrapping it around my legs. We laugh about it now."

Coal strikes added to the problem, as did new government regulations on power plant emissions the pioneers would never have imagined. Earl Johnson called this era his "most disappointing time" in an interview conducted just before his retirement in 1982. He explained himself in this way:

"We receive most of our power from Dairyland Cooperatives' power plants in Alma and Genoa, Wisconsin. When the Clean Air Act and the Occupational Safety and Health Administration (OSHA) went into effect, new stacks had to be built at Alma and a different type of coal had to be hauled in, one with a low sulfur concentration. We were required to use Western coal from Wyoming instead of West Virginia or Illinois coal, and we were affected two ways. Wyoming coal had to be brought in by trains, and the transportation cost was higher. And Wyoming coal generates comparatively less energy per ton, so more tons had to be brought in to produce the same amount of energy as before."

Manager Bruce Meistad, right, joined Ace Telephone CEO John Owens, left, and Rod Morcomb, standing, to sign documents as the cooperative began offering cell phone service.

He pointed out that wholesale power costs when he started working for the cooperative in 1941 amounted to fifty cents of every dollar in revenue. With the increases taking effect, that figure was now seventy-five cents.

Rates were on the rise. Americans felt the pinch, and Tri-County's members were no exception. "Our problems started when the first oil embargo hit," Spartz recalled. "After that was when you saw rates moving to meet expenses. On the other side of the same coin, this co-op was always big on load control. We offered rebates on water heaters so we could control peaks. We were pushing electric water heaters and of course you could control that, too."

Tri-County had always pushed energy efficiency. In response to the energy crisis of the 1970s, the cooperative stepped up its efforts to help members keep their electric bills in line.

One highlight of the decade was the election of Tri-County's first woman director. Naomi Fruechte joined the board in 1978. She would not be the last woman elected to the co-op's board, however. Judith A. Sikkink was elected in

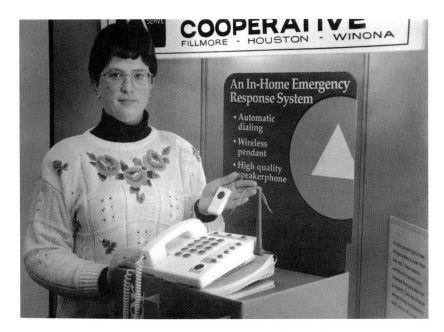

Above left: *Joy Henderson shows off the In-Home Emergency Response System marketed by the cooperative. Tri-County continues to offer security services to members through Heartland Security.*

Above right: *Members in need of an electric grill could get one from Tri-County, as demonstrated by Mary Rislove. The co-op also sold electric thermal storage heating units and other electrical equipment not carried by other local businesses.*

1989 and served until 2007. Patricia VanGundy came on the board in 2005 and continues to serve. And Jenny Scharmer, who joined the board in 2006 when her father, Jerome Gernes, did not seek re-election, is currently the board chair.

Another milestone was the addition of computers to handle payroll, accounting, and billing. Lorraine Benson can remember when everything at the cooperative was done by hand. She started working for Tri-County in its Billing Department in December 1963.

"Everything was done manually," she remembers. "We had a Burroughs billing machine at that time. Every member had their own paper ledger sheet. And we would sit together at billing day with big charts overhead and an adding machine at our side. We would put a ledger sheet with their name on and key in a dollar amount. We looked up what they would be charged based on their kilowatts."

There was a lot to keep track of. Ledgers were wheeled around on big metal carts, sorted alphabetically and by account type, for example: single-phase, city resident, and commercial accounts. Some members received a credit for letting the co-op control their water heater during times of peak use.

"Even back then, there were always questions about why the bills were so high. They could ask, 'Could there be something wrong?'"

Asked when computers came on board, Lorraine could not remember. "It's not something I've even tried to remember," she said, recalling the steep learning curve for the new technology. At first, Tri-County used computers linked to servers at Dairyland Power. Later, they switched to Central Area Data Processing Cooperative, now the National Information Solutions Cooperative, or NISC, based in St. Louis.

While those learning to use the new machines might have grumbled a little at first, they quickly learned that this was a big improvement over the billing machines and big Underwood typewriters previously used. "They were totally silent," Lorraine said of the computers. "That was the best thing. Because those Burroughs billing machines, they would go clunk, clunk, clunk and they were so loud. You had to be careful if you were a woman not to get your necklace caught in them."

After forty-two years of service to Tri-County, Earl Johnson would retire on October 31, 1982. But first, he would oversee the construction of a new office building, the first for the cooperative that was designed from the ground up as an electric cooperative facility.

In 1978, the cooperative had purchased land in Rushford from Tri-County Oil. Since that time, plans had been drawn up taking into account each employee's needs. A groundbreaking was held in August 1981, with completion expected by May of the following year.

The new facility, located on Jessie Street, would be almost twice as large as the one it replaced, with 18,750 square feet of usable space. Energy efficiency was stressed, with insulation adequate to meet the Minnesota winters installed. A community room on the lower level was made available to local groups when it wasn't hosting employee or director meetings.

Upon its completion, Johnson would remark, "We really didn't know how crowded we were until we moved into this spacious building. Over the thirty years that we occupied the old facility, every nook and corner had been put to use."

Board President Harvey Rislow shows some Christmas spirit as he helps decorate the office. Rislow served on the co-op board for many years.

One of Tri-County's long-time employees was Rocky Carlson, who retired as engineering and operations supervisor.

Upon Johnson's retirement, the board tapped a long-time member of the rural electric family as its next manager. Bruce Meistad, a thirty-three-year-old Wisconsin native, was "born into cooperatives" as a newspaper headline put it after his hiring was announced. Bruce's father managed several electric cooperatives, prompting his son to plan for a career in rural electrification.

He was a new breed of manager who knew more about the financial side of things than line construction. Previous managers of Tri-County Electric were local boys who grew up on farms and were perhaps more comfortable working outside than in the office. Bruce would break that mold, being an outsider and college-educated, with a degree in business administration and accounting from the University of Wisconsin-Eau Claire. He worked for the IRS for two years before joining the staff of Riverland Energy Cooperative. He later moved to Trempealeau Electric Cooperative, another system in the Dairyland family of cooperatives, where he was assistant manager.

Meistad set improving communications with members as one of his first priorities, given that most members at the time didn't remember the days before electricity came to the countryside and perhaps didn't understand how a cooperative works.

Computers dramatically changed the way the cooperative operated when they were first introduced. Here engineer/draftsman Verle Ramsey gets some instruction on their operation from Sara Krage.

The new manager settled into the new facilities and took the cooperative through a turbulent period of rising rates and a decline in membership due to the farm crisis of the 1980s. His message to the members in the *Light Conversation* newsletter often stressed measures being taken at the cooperative to hold down expenses during a time when wholesale power costs were escalating.

For nineteen years he managed the cooperative until tragedy struck. On February 7, 2001, Meistad was leading a safety meeting at the cooperative office when he collapsed and died of an apparent heart attack. He was fifty-one years old.

"He was a wonderful man, very intelligent and easygoing, a soft-spoken person," said Kaye Bernard, Tri-County's vice president of finance and administration/CFO. "It was quite a shock. We all knew at some point he wanted to look at retirement and would be leaving. He figured five more years and he'd be ready to retire. We just never knew he would be gone so soon."

A tragedy such as the one that occurred with the manager's death could have severely set back the cooperative's operations. Instead, thanks to the management style of Bruce Meistad, the employees were able to mourn his passing and still get the job done.

"I think we were very fortunate that the management leadership that Bruce had was really hands-on," said Brian Krambeer, who would assume the reins as manager just a week after the tragedy took place. "It was more of a goal and directive leadership style, that all of the department managers—we basically took care of running the day-to-day operations. Because of that management style, we were very successful in continuing to move forward."

The new manager was a relative newcomer to Tri-County at the time. A native of Waukon, Iowa, he became the cooperative's coordinator of marketing and business development in May 1997 after spending ten years as the member service and marketing director for Clay-Union Electric Cooperative in Vermillion, South Dakota. He had recently been promoted to manager of member services and marketing for Tri-County.

Freddie Arnold was construction supervisor when this photo was published in the co-op's annual report.

With Brian Krambeer at the helm, Tri-County began a long process of strategic planning that would pay huge dividends in the years to come. He would forge alliances with neighboring municipalities and cooperatives that would help both sides prosper. He would position Tri-County for possible deregulation and the potential loss of service it might bring. And his strong leadership would see the cooperative through one of its darkest periods and into a new era of strength and commitment to community.

Bruce Meistad joined the board for this dinner function during his reign as the co-op's manager. His untimely death during a safety meeting stunned the employees. However, his management style left the cooperative in excellent shape during the transition.

Chapter 7 —
Tri-County's Finest Hour

On Saturday, August 18, 2007, a strange weather pattern greeted southeast Minnesota. All day long, a warm front extended across northern Iowa and central Illinois, where it would remain through Sunday. A very moist and warm air mass rose up and over this boundary, providing the fuel for showers and thunderstorms. Due to the depth of the warm layer, and the considerable amount of moisture in the air, the stage was set for unprecedented heavy rainfall across the Upper Mississippi Valley.

Much of downtown Rushford, including Tri-County's headquarters, was still underwater when this photo was taken from the air.

Thunderstorms developed on Saturday, eventually orienting into a west-to-east-moving line from the northern plains, through southern Minnesota, and then into southwest Wisconsin Saturday night. Tri-County Electric's headquarters in Rushford was directly in the path of the most favorable area for heavy rain. When the rains came—and continued to fall for twenty-four hours—they would present the cooperative with its most daunting challenge since its creation.

Previous page: *Employees survey the damage to Tri-County's fleet of vehicles in the wake of the flood. Virtually the entire fleet was destroyed. Photo by Jon Sobeich.*

Only the tops of vehicles parked next to the warehouse can be seen following heavy flooding in August 2007. Photo by Jon Sobeich.

Before the sky cleared, two-thirds of Rushford was covered in water as Rush Creek topped its protective levees. In places water surged to eight feet deep. Two city wells were submerged. The town's wastewater treatment plant was wiped out. Cell phone towers were down. Seventy homes were demolished. A few employees' homes were significantly damaged. Fifty-eight Rushford businesses suffered losses, and the storm caused a total of $71 million in damages. Tri-County's office, warehouse, fleet, and inventory suffered $6 million in damages plus another $1 million in damage to washed-out distribution lines.

When the water finally receded, it left behind three to five inches of toxic muck and a community wondering where to begin the restoration effort.

It would require a superhuman effort to recover from this disaster, but like gold tested in fire, Tri-County's employees and members alike would witness what can honestly be called the cooperative's "finest hour." Their achievement is even more notable given the disaster many faced at home.

No resident of the area had ever seen rain fall like it did in those two days. In many areas, from one to two inches and more per hour fell, and continued to fall. Before the rain let up on Sunday, seventeen inches would fall in some parts of the region. Once gentle creeks and streams turned into raging rivers, devouring everything in their paths, with the first reports of flooding coming in at 6 p.m. Record flooding took place, with the Root River reaching 18.75 feet, eclipsing the earlier record of 18.32 feet set in 1965.

By 8 p.m., a mudslide had closed Highway 76 between Money Creek and Houston. Dozens of other mudslides and washouts would make travel by road all but impossible in the coming hours. In addition, several cars were swept off roads. In all, seven people lost their lives in the tragedy.

Staking engineer Jeff Hoiland examines power lines damaged by the flood. The fast-moving water caused heavy damage to Tri-County's lines and left close to 4,000 without power. The repair bill for the lines alone was more than $1 million.

Back in Rushford, employees of Tri-County Electric abandoned weekend plans and headed to the office, knowing the weather would lead to outages. Mike Ebner was one of the first on the scene, arriving at 3 a.m. Sunday morning. He watched as a wall of water breached the city's dikes and surged through the streets.

Besides serving as Rushford's fire department chief, Ebner is also Tri-County's line superintendent. Between calls to coordinate the fire department's emergency response, he called Tri-County Manager Brian Krambeer with these words: "I said, 'Brian, Tri-County is under water.'"

Krambeer met line workers Keith Pederson and Joe Jordan at the office and the three waded through waist-deep water to get to the warehouse where Tri-County's fleet of trucks was stored. The three knew that when the cooperative mounted its outage recovery effort, these trucks would be crucial to making repairs.

Pederson recalls forcing his way through chest-high water as he attempted to open the rear door of the warehouse. Unfortunately, the door required two keys and he only had one. Instead, he worked his way to the front door, which was secured by a combination lock.

Above: *Manager Brian Krambeer, left, explains the recovery operation to Senator Norm Coleman at the Rushford Red Cross shelter. The area was later declared a disaster area, opening the door to federal assistance.*

Right: *This storage area in the headquarters basement was completely underwater from the flood. Many valuable records were damaged, although some were able to be restored.*

In the street in front of the co-op headquarters, a flooded police car sat, its lights flashing on as its electronics shorted out. The lock was already underwater, but Pederson's blind attempts at entering the combination worked and the door opened.

The two line workers found the co-op's pickups and cars fully submerged. The digger derrick and bucket trucks became their main focus. As they opened doors, the water surged inside. Only one of the twenty-five vehicles would start. The rest were a total loss.

Other employees found routes to the office through the flood and began trying to fish equipment from the rising water. They were literally diving into the water in the search for tools. Little could be saved, and most of what was plucked from the water would not be serviceable for long. For example, tool belts retrieved in the early hours quickly grew mold. "I don't know what was in that water," said Bob Spartz, "but it was so corrosive that a lot of the stuff you couldn't use. We salvaged what we could."

Besides wrecking the office and warehouse in Rushford, the flood took out miles of line and other equipment, causing a "flood" of outages. "I believe right after the flood, the number of members without power was 3,300 to 4,000," Spartz said. "With a limited number of equipment, a lot of guys used their personal equipment. Within days or so acquaintances I have within the cooperative family in the state called me and said, 'We heard Rushford had problems and if you need anything give us a call.' So some of our neighbors had vehicles coming immediately."

Added Ted Kjos, vice president of marketing and external relations, "Our inventory really took a hit. Damage was devastating and almost complete. There was very little left to work with for resale or to help us in our work. We had just received a shipment of smart meters. Some of that I had waited almost a year to get."

Debris removed from the warehouse awaits collection behind the building. The warehouse was back in service in about a month.

Another crisis was the damage to computers that did everything from billing to accounting to payroll. "We lost all of our computers and our servers," said Kaye Bernard. "The entire basement content was a loss. That was devastating. Our initial concern was backup. A couple items we did save were rack mounted and high but they weren't needed because we did have backups."

Fortunately, cooperatives are seldom alone. Tri-County contracts for data processing services with the National Information Solutions Cooperative, a Missouri-based data processing cooperative. One call to NISC got the ball rolling to restore vital computer services to Tri-County. "We are so fortunate that we are affiliated with an organization like them," Kaye said. "One call to their organization made that morning from a cell phone at the side of the road at the Rushford airport was all it took. Within an hour we had employees rebuilding our servers, packing up equipment, and leaving their Mandan, North Dakota office to come to Rushford. They were in the office the next day with all the equipment we needed to get us back up and going again."

Dairyland also came to the rescue, proving the value of the relationship created so many years ago when Tri-County became part of the G&T. Dairyland employees Lance Burke and Steve Schroeder were particularly helpful. "They did

a lot for us," recalled Spartz. "We didn't have any two-way communications, didn't have radios. Steve came up and gave us a hand-held so we could have communications with other guys.

"Lance started calling around to get any extra equipment he could. We didn't have any digger derricks or bucket trucks. We needed bucket trucks more than anything, and we also needed crawler units to get through rain-soaked areas and mudslides."

A tractor pulls one of the flooded trucks out of the warehouse after the water had receded. Crews working in the early hours attempted to save these trucks but only succeeded in one case. The entire fleet had to be replaced.

In addition to Dairyland, aid poured in from People's Cooperative Services, Rochester; Dakota Electric Association, Farmington; Freeborn-Mower Cooperative Services, Albert Lea; Wisconsin-based Adams-Columbia Electric Cooperative, Friendship and Riverland Energy Cooperative, Arcadia; and Iowa's Hawkeye Rural Electric Cooperative, Cresco. Adams-Columbia was able to provide five bucket trucks the cooperative had intended to trade in on new vehicles but had not released yet.

All electric cooperatives plan for emergencies. An emergency preparedness plan is as common to today's electric cooperative as the bucket trucks used to service lines. Tri-County was no exception. In fact, its staff had recently met to rehearse various crisis situations and fine-tune the procedures that were crucial to the recovery.

"A disaster plan has to cover everything," said Krambeer. "One of the benefits of having a plan is everyone knows you have a plan, everyone knows their role, and it serves as a resource to go to when everything else is gone. But we never anticipated losing the office, the warehouse, the fleet, the inventory, and everything else. I really encourage co-ops when they go through their disaster plan to ask, 'How do we start over?'"

Added Spartz, "When we did our disaster planning, we always figured the worst disaster would be a tornado and we might lose either the office or the shop. But we never figured we'd lose everything. We did lose everything. You know, you're faced with that and it's horrendous, but everyone got into the mindset that we've got a job to do; it's different than it was before but we still want to get the job done. But when people are down and out they put their best foot forward, and there's no complaining. Everyone does what it takes to get the job done."

He was one of the employees who had damage at home, with a foundation that caved in. "A number of us were in the same boat," he said. "After awhile, you become a zombie. You come in and go to work, you go home and go to work. You knew what needed to be done and you did it. Now you look back and you say, 'Holy cow, that was a lot of work.'"

Ginny Johnson, Tri-County's executive administrative secretary, logs items salvaged from the office by Ted Kjos.

Showing the leadership skills that prompted the board into naming him manager, Krambeer quickly rallied the troops. At first, the plan was to set up operations at the Caledonia outpost. Within hours of the flood, restoration of service began from this office with dispatch operations under Jerry Gudmundson's leadership. Calls began pouring in from members without power. Gudmundson estimated that the cooperative received 2,400 calls from August 18 to 22.

However, it quickly became apparent that employees needed to be involved with the recovery effort in Rushford, ground zero for the disaster. Within twenty-four hours, emergency operations were moved to the Rushford Municipal Airport. A hanger was pressed into service to store salvaged equipment and as a staging area once new materials began to arrive. And a modular home that served as the airport's lounge was converted into the temporary Tri-County headquarters.

Two days after the flood, Tri-County began conducting business from the airport. The kitchen doubled as engineering and operations. The manager shared the den with other department heads. Billing and accounting took over the living room. Most of the important documents and supplies were kept at the airport hanger. Members could once again come in and pay bills. Meanwhile, dispatching continued to operate out of the Caledonia warehouse.

"Members were surprised at how cozy it was," said Susie Norby, member service rep. "I guess they were amazed what we were doing with the space we had. And that we were already up and running."

Throughout the disaster, Brenda Tesch directed communications to keep members informed of restoration progress. Getting the message out to people was difficult because of the lack of ways to communicate. Phone lines were down. Travel was difficult if not impossible. Internet service had not been restored and cell phone service was spotty.

"Every morning, myself and two other employees made calls to radio stations," Tesch said. "They put us on live and talked with us about our situation. At the end of every interview they would tell us if anything changes or you need to get an update out, just give us a call."

Added Brian Krambeer, "Communication is critical in a disaster, not just for our membership and the general public, but also to let our employees know

Tri-County's Operation Round-Up program, which lets members round their bills up to the next highest number, contributed funds that bought two pumps that helped residents remove water from their basements.

what is going on. We started doing weekly employee meetings to let everyone know what was going on but equally important, because our employees are out there talking to our members and bringing back information."

After thirty days of working out of the lounge and warehouse, it was time to move back downtown. The Rushford warehouse had been cleaned and sanitized and five warehouse office areas were reconfigured to accommodate eighteen people. Another nineteen employees moved into a four-plex construction trailer parked behind the ruined office. Plastic totes were moved in so employees could work with material that survived.

Like a Phoenix rising from some soggy ashes, Tri-County Electric suffered through a period of tight quarters and low inventory. Those employees who lost their homes found assistance pouring in from electric cooperatives across the nation as fast as the floodwaters did.

Tesch helped set up an employee assistance fund and handed out checks to those who were in harm's way. "The donations and generosity will never be forgotten by those people," she said. "I got to hand out some of those checks and see tears in their eyes when they got those checks. I cannot describe that gratitude."

One employee summed it up by saying he had always understood what it meant to be part of a cooperative family since he had worked there so long, but until the flood, his family hadn't understood what that meant. They do now.

An emergency plan is always a work in progress. Tri-County gained valuable insight into what works and what doesn't in a disaster. Through it all, the response from employees was key to turning a crisis situation into a truly remarkable recovery.

Mike Ebner was one of the Tri-County employees whose home suffered heavy damage from the flood. The missing drywall shows just how high the floodwaters got. Many employees worked the flood recovery at work, then had to face the same situation when they returned home.

Employee spirits stayed high despite working in cramped conditions in the temporary office building located at the Rushford airport.

Chapter 8—
The Year of Recovery and Beyond

They say for every dark cloud, there's a silver lining. For Tri-County Electric Cooperative, the silver lining would appear on September 29, 2008, the first day of business in a new office located at 31110 Cooperative Way. Long before the Great Flood of 2007, Tri-County was once again feeling the need for new office space. In fact, at a strategic planning meeting held in 2004, the need for a new headquarters building was identified by the board. The physical growth of the staff, in addition to the use of new technology never dreamed of when the current building was erected, would hinder the staff in their attempt to provide the level of service expected by a twenty-first-century membership.

Tri-County crews traveled to Paducah, Kentucky, to help with power restoration in the wake of a devastating 2009 ice storm. Pictured from left to right are Tim Anderson, Tyler Eide, Steve Oian, and Davin Thompson.

Slowly, the board and management advanced plans for the new structure. Following a site evaluation survey in the Rushford area, the board approved purchasing twenty-five acres of land just off Highway 16 outside the village. Plans for the new building were in the

Previous page: *Tyler Eide works on a line in the Winnebago Valley. Southeast Minnesota's scenic landscape is often a challenge for the co-op's crews.*

Tri-County lent a hand to neighboring Hawkeye Electric out of Cresco, Iowa, following an ice storm there. Cooperation among cooperatives is one of the cooperative principles electric co-ops follow.

works when disaster, in the form of the 2007 flood, occurred. In a few short hours, the headquarters, warehouse, and the entire fleet of trucks were destroyed. But as the recovery effort rolled forward, that advanced planning began to pay off. Construction on the new headquarters could begin in earnest while the staff made do in temporary quarters.

The recovery effort would be greatly assisted by nearly $2.3 million from the Federal Emergency Management Agency, a 90-percent forgivable loan of $2.4 million from the Minnesota Department of Employment and Economic Development, and a $5-million disaster recovery loan amortized over thirty years from the Rural Utilities Service.

The site would offer safer access to two highways for the cooperative's big trucks and pole trailers. Prompted by the flood experience, a study was commissioned that showed the site was above the 500-year-flood projection level. For the first time in its history, the cooperative's pole yard was now located on site. Having poles and other materials nearby allows quick access and a secure location for storage.

From the beginning, the new headquarters was designed to be a model of energy efficiency and efficient operation. First, the building is situated to maximize the use of natural lighting during daylight hours. The Service Center blocks the harsh northwest winds, while the office space faces south to allow for passive solar heat gain.

Landscaping was designed around native plants that don't need frequent watering. Grass was planted only in the area closest to the building, again to reduce maintenance.

Concrete, instead of asphalt, was used on the parking areas to reduce the "heat island" effect. Runoff rainwater from the building, parking, and storage areas is collected and diverted to a holding pond on the south side of the building.

Constant preparation makes a big difference during times of crisis, Tri-County's board and management believe. That philosophy paid off during the Great Flood of 2007. Shown here are some of the key staff taking part in an emergency simulation in January 2007, eight months before the flood. From left to right are Mark Zweibohmer, Jerry Gudmundson, Kaye Bernard, Brian Krambeer, Ginny Johnson, Mike Ebner, and Ted Kjos. In the right corner is Bob Spartz.

Outside lighting is all directed downward. This allows the building to be lighted for security, but reduces light spilling into the night skies and off site.

During the flood, the need for water during and after disaster situations was recognized, so a pump house and a 65,000-gallon storage tank were added, along with attachments for fire hoses.

The efficiency concept continues on the inside. The polished concrete floors give the impression of expensive granite but require little maintenance, and fewer harsh chemical cleaners. Paint with low volatile organic compounds was used throughout the building, benefiting both those applying the paint and the employees working inside.

Above left: *Groundbreaking for Tri-County's new state-of-the-art office building took place in 2007. Shown here, from left to right, are State Representative Gene Pelowski along with Tri-County directors Roger Hegland, Patty VanGundy, Jenny Scharmer, and Ron Stevens.*

Above right: *Gordon Johnson, Tri-County's metering/energy control foreman, sets up one of the first "smart meters" on the co-op's lines. These meters send readings back to the co-op automatically and allow members to access use history via the Internet.*

Wherever possible, recycled materials were used for construction. This starts at the reception area inside the front door, which is made from recycled metals. Workstations were made from a recycled laminate and include corkboards made from recycled materials.

New Homeland Security standards were used in designing the building's security system. Employees carry pass cards that allow them access to interior office space. Cameras also monitor hallways and sensitive areas throughout the interior and exterior of the building. This helps keep employees and visitors safe and helps deter vandalism and theft.

Dual-function bathroom flushing mechanisms and low-flow showerheads and faucets reduce the amount of water used. Lighting is kept to a minimum, with just enough lights in the hallways so that you can find your way. Bright lights are limited to placement directly over work areas where they are needed the most. Careful placement of lighting is designed to save on energy costs, a model other businesses can follow.

Motion sensors control lights in seldom-used locations, while other areas are programmed to turn on and off during and after working hours. All lighting can also be manually turned off if needed.

Every form of energy-saving technology possible was designed into the building. This includes the white-painted roof, which helps lower cooling costs by reflecting sunlight away from the building. Ground-source heat pumps use the earth's nearly constant temperature for heating and cooling at the lowest possible cost. As with the lighting, automatic controls raise and lower the temperature to allow for greater efficiency.

A Wellness Room, designed to promote healthy living habits for employees, was added. As a bonus, access to exercise equipment meets one of the criteria for the cooperative reducing the cost of its medical insurance premiums.

Recycling doesn't stop with the green building materials used. In the service area there are large bins for recycling paper, cardboard, plastics, and aluminum. With employees sorting their own materials and producing less waste, the cooperative also saves on trash-removal costs.

Johnson's Rolling Acres built a new dairy facility in 2000, incorporating many new energy efficiency measures into the design. Dairy farmers were early supporters of rural electrification and continue to benefit from having access to affordable and reliable power. Shown here are Mark Johnson, Brad Johnson, Gerald Eide, LeRoy Johnson, and Richard Johnson.

Advanced technology can be found in the new board room. The building is equipped with wireless Internet service and many built-in features for advanced presentation requirements. This allows staff to take part in Web conferences, reducing the need for travel to meetings. In addition, all data is backed up off site and encrypted for personal information protection.

Should disaster strike again, an on-site generator can power the entire headquarters. Another plus is that the cooperative can take the building off line during times of peak energy use for added savings for every member.

A new Operations Center allows projection of the complete system map, always up to date in a way that the old printed wall maps could not allow. State-of-the-art communications help speed outage recovery.

Finally, the Service Center allows the entire fleet of vehicles to be parked inside. The advantage of this is apparent to anyone who has tried to get inside a parked car in the wake of an ice storm. The Service Center was designed

Every aspect of the new headquarters building was carefully considered, including the dispatch center. Pictured are Audra Skalet and Jerry Gudmundson.

so that trucks can be parked close to materials for easy loading when the day begins. Wireless Internet was also included here so that on-board computers in trucks would have access to the needed information.

Many other features were built in to position the cooperative for opportunities down the road and to serve as a solid base for serving the membership for many years to come. Since its completion, the building has played host to groups from electric cooperatives around the country that are planning new offices.

Besides the office serving as a model for other electric cooperatives to follow, Tri-County's experience during the flood has helped other cooperatives prepare for potential disasters. Several members of the staff have spoken at meetings around the country, sharing insight on organizing line crews, handling public relations, and working with FEMA and other government agencies in the aftermath.

"I have had the privilege of going all over the country speaking on the disaster recovery," said Manager Brian Krambeer. "I have unofficially been told that this co-op set the model for others to follow in dealing with a disaster, which is very flattering."

Not only did the staff move into brand new office space, the line workers who toil in the field would receive an entire fleet of new vehicles. Long-time outside employees must have felt like kids at Christmas when the shiny new vehicles, featuring the latest in safety equipment, rolled up.

"You would be hard-pressed to say there is a cooperative that has better equipment than we do," said Bob Spartz. "Who else can say all their equipment is new?"

While it can take an entire year to spec and bid out a new truck, Spartz put together a standardized bid that called for identical digger derrick and bucket trucks. "Crews can get in any truck and regardless, everything is the same. If you can run one, you can run them all," Spartz said.

Little by little, computers are being added to trucks. This lets crews access member information to speed response time and ensure that the correct materials are loaded on the truck. "That technology, it's probably the biggest change," Spartz said of his forty-plus years at the co-op. "We still build line the same way we used to. We've still got to go out and physically set poles and all those things. But we have better equipment to set poles, better equipment to string lines. The equipment has improved, but so has the technology in the office. And the end result, it's all for the betterment of the member."

Electric co-ops were born in politics and they will die there without constant vigilance. Tri-County Manager Brian Krambeer and Minnesota Rural Electric Association representative Lee Sundberg discussed rural electric issues with U.S. Representative Gil Gutnecht during a visit in 2006.

The Great Flood of 2007 wasn't the only crisis Tri-County faced in the new millennium, but the one that ushered in the year 2000 proved to be a non-event. Across the country, businesses worked feverishly to update computer systems and hardware in anticipation of the Y2K bug. The concern came when computer programmers discovered that a memory-saving programming technique—writing the year without the first two digits—could lead to loss of data and computer confusion when the year rolled over to 2000. Any program that used year information would have trouble distinguishing between 1900 and 2000, it was believed.

The problem was first discovered in 1985, giving the industry time to fix the problem. "I was on call that night," Kaye Bernard recalled. "We did all our preparations and I sat up all night to see if anything would happen. And it didn't. It was scary. Because who knew what was going to happen? It was the same as any virus scare that comes along. You can't pass it off. You got to take it seriously, to a point."

Added Lorraine Benson, "It was a concern, not a huge concern, but it was there. We were so thankful afterwards. They didn't have to make us worry that much."

In its seventy-five years of history, much has changed for the staff of the cooperative. Gone are the obnoxious typewriters and billing machines from the early days. In their place is a computer system that allows Tri-County employees to digitally archive every document. Once, a courier carried bags of checks to the bank at the end of every working day. Today those checks are scanned and a data file is sent to the bank for deposit.

Even though the goal of area coverage was reached many years ago, Tri-County continues to improve service, using loans from the Rural Utilities Service, the agency that replaced the Rural Electrification Administration in 1994. In this photo, Tri-County receives approval of a $9.5-million loan for new line and upgrades. From left to right are U.S. Representative Gil Gutnecht, Director Jeff Redalen, Director Patty VanGundy, RUS Field Representative Kris Stanley, Director Allen Aarsvold, and staff assistant to Senator Norm Coleman Gerald Woodley. At front, signing the check, is USDA Rural Development State Director Steve Wenzel (left) and Tri-County president/CEO Brian Krambeer (right).

Members no longer have to read their own meters now that the cooperative has completed work on installing automated meters, or AMR. The meters offer more than the convenience of automatic readings. When a member has a high bill complaint, employees can show their daily energy use. This can help pinpoint problems or at least show areas where energy conservation may be improved.

Members can now access this information via a Web portal from Tri-County's Web site, www.TEC.coop. They can also pay bills online and find more information about the cooperative's many services.

The work of those in the field also has changed dramatically from the days when the Arnold brothers strung the lines for Tri-County. What used to take hours can now be done much faster with hydraulic tools, high-reaching bucket trucks, and go-anywhere four-wheel drive.

Much of the work today is done energized. "Nowadays, unless it's something critical, you don't even de-energize a line," Spartz said. "We are dealing with different clientele today. They walk in a room and flip a switch, they want it to work. Whereas, the mom-and-pop farmer, if it didn't work, they might sit a day before they called you. It's just a change of times. Back in the early days, you didn't have that much that you used electric for. You take a farm operation today, without electricity, they are pretty much at a standstill."

Sometimes, however, the landscape of Tri-County's service area forces a return to the old ways or perhaps some creative thinking. That was the case in the fall of 2008, when journeyman linemen Tyler Eide, Davin Thompson, Tim Anderson, and foreman Andy Prinsen needed to raise a line above an historic dam on the Root River at Lanesboro. The crew used a fishing pole to cast across the cold, swift-flowing stream, then attached a rope and finally the power line.

During Farm Safety Day, 400 fourth-graders representing twelve schools spent the day in Mabel learning about safety. Tri-County's Assistant Member Services Director Brad Pecinovsky taught electric safety during the event.

The dam was built before the Civil War, and used to power a mill that served the community. Since 1954, it has supplied the city's municipal utility with 230 kilowatts of hydropower. Tri-County did the work under a maintenance agreement with the municipal. The cooperative provides wholesale power to eight municipal systems and is the retail supplier to four others.

"We provide electricity to them and work very closely with those communities," Krambeer said. "We not only help them with the management of their electric system, but also assist with economic development and energy efficiency programs that they would like to roll out."

In 2001, seven of these municipal systems signed new twenty-year agreements with the cooperative. Five years later, Rushford became the eighth wholesale customer. Some of these systems began taking power from Tri-County as early as 1946.

Because of this cooperation and a special wholesale rate from Dairyland Power, Tri-County has avoided the cooperative-versus-municipal territory squabbles that have plagued the rest of Minnesota. Since 1974, twenty-nine of the state's forty-four distribution cooperatives have lost territory to municipals that annexed surrounding land.

The cooperative's relationship with towns in its service area has benefited residents in other ways. As co-op customers, the municipals gain access to economic development capital from the Department of Agriculture's Rural Economic Development Loans and Grants program. Over the years, more than $1.7 million in loans have been directed into the local economy.

One beneficiary of this service was Caledonia's Sno Pac Foods. The family business received $650,000 in loans over ten years, which were used to update production lines and replace forty-year-old machinery at its food-packing plant.

Another economic development loan resulted in Tri-County's largest load, jobs for local residents, and a better return on corn grown by area farmers. Local farmers who are members of Tri-County Electric formed Pro-Corn, LLC in 1998 to make ethanol from corn. Tri-County and Dairyland teamed up to land a $200,000 loan for the group in 1998 and an additional $300,000 in 2002.

Through an agreement with the city of Preston, Tri-County serves the ethanol plant through a city substation. The 8-megawatt load helps keep costs down for all of Tri-County's members.

Tri-County has found other ways to help small towns thrive. The co-op handles all of the billing for two of their wholesale cities—including trash collection, water, sewer, and electricity charges—through a billing system designed by data processing cooperative NISC. Residents receive a single billing statement printed at Dairyland's printing service. The co-op collects the money and then transfers it to the city's account.

In addition, Tri-County is constantly looking for ways to partner with other cooperatives to hold down operating costs. For example, engineering services are shared between Tri-County and three other electric cooperatives in Iowa. The cooperatives also share a safety coordinator and an arborist for their right-of-way maintenance programs.

This "cooperation among cooperatives" went even further when the board of Iowa's Hawkeye Electric in nearby Cresco, Iowa, asked Krambeer to manage the cooperative while the board considered its options for filling a manager vacancy. Both cooperatives' boards thought the relationship would be a good one. Since that time, the contract has been extended twice. Krambeer splits time between the two systems in the same way George Werner managed both an electric and a

Since 1990, Tri-County has cleaned up trash along a two-mile stretch of Highway 16 near Rushford as part of Minnesota's Adopt-A-Highway program.

telephone cooperative in the past. Ted Kjos, Tri-County's vice president of marketing and external relations, also shares time with the Iowa cooperative.

Tri-County's members have access to other services besides electricity from their cooperative. One of these is a load-management program that lets Dairyland Power shut off non-essential appliances such as water heaters, irrigation, and commercial loads for short periods of time when demand for electricity is at its highest. Because the load controls are cycled off for only a short period of time, most members never notice.

"It helps members control the cost of electricity and use energy wisely," said Ted Kjos, who added that Tri-County employees have "energy efficiency stamped on our foreheads."

"Through load control, we are delaying the need for the next power plant," Kjos said. "We can control load a lot cheaper than building the next power plant."

Tri-County has the largest amount of load under control on the Dairyland system, with 8,000 water heaters, 1,800 heating systems, and sixty commercial or industrial accounts controlled.

Tri-County gave out thirty-two "Kill A Watt" energy use monitors to sixteen local libraries in 2010. These are loaned to patrons interested in improving the energy efficiency of their homes. Shown here are Annie Hoiland, Tri-County's communications specialist, and Elizabeth Gibson-Gasset from the Houston Public Library.

Efforts to help members control their electric bills include information printed in the *Light Conversation* newsletter and on the Web site, in addition to participation in a Home Energy Expo where contractors are taught the latest in energy efficiency. In addition, employees have worked with area schools, businesses, and farms to reduce energy use.

Part of this huge push came when Minnesota passed a state law mandating new energy efficiency standards. State law also requires utilities to invest in renewable generation resources. Through Dairyland, Tri-County and other member systems are ahead of schedule in meeting the state's 25 percent renewables by the year 2025 mandate. Dairyland is using a combination of wind, biomass, landfill gas-to-energy, and manure digesters to generate this green power.

Other services offered by the cooperative came in response to deregulation of the electricity industry by some states. Deregulation was supposed to do for the power industry what it did for the airline and telecommunications industries: bring consumers lower prices and more competition. Instead, utility bills rose sharply for residents

in seventeen states that deregulated. Fortunately, Minnesota's legislators wisely decided on a "wait and see" policy for deregulation, and the state remained regulated. But utilities were encouraged to diversify their services in response to this legislative push.

Tri-County partnered with other cooperatives to offer services ranging from home security to propane supply. Members could also buy heating products such as boilers and thermal storage systems that were not readily available elsewhere. Despite this push to diversify, Tri-County remained focused on its core business, supplying electricity. Other services were carefully tailored to minimize risk and to avoid competing with local businesses.

Brenda Tesch, Tri-County's public relations director, and Iyla Mulvenna, Caledonia Food Shelf director, show off a program that offered members a free CFL light bulb in return for a donation to area food pantries in March 2010. The program resulted in 191 members donating 882 items along with $1,397 in cash to food shelves in Caledonia, Preston, St. Charles, Spring Valley, Rushford, Winona, and Wykoff.

Heartland Security, which offers medical and security monitoring, is owned by Tri-County and twelve other electric cooperatives in Minnesota and Iowa. More than 4,000 people use its services. Tri-County became a one-stop energy supplier when it formed SELECTUS Energy to provide propane in its service area. Today, the propane subsidiary is partnered with Country Comfort.

As Tri-County Electric Cooperative approaches its seventy-fifth year, a lot has changed and a lot remains the same. New technologies have improved the way the cooperative does business. Yet, that business still is conducted with the seven cooperative principles in mind. The focus remains on providing affordable and reliable electricity to members.

It can be said that electric cooperatives were born in politics and they will die in politics unless close attention is paid to what happens in the state and national capitals. The future of Tri-County Electric and its sister cooperatives across the country today are tied to a debate taking place in Washington, D.C.

In the summer of 2010, Congress was debating an energy bill that could include climate change legislation. States such as Minnesota that rely on coal to generate most of their electricity have much at stake in this debate.

Coal remains by far the most economical way to generate electricity. The United States also enjoys a tremendous reserve of low-sulfur coal in western states such as Wyoming. Yet, efforts to restrict releases of carbon dioxide could make it expensive to continue to generate with coal.

This has cooperative officials worried, and prompted the start of the "Our Energy, Our Future" campaign by the National Rural Electric Cooperative Association. Through this effort, more than 1.3 million messages were sent to Congress by electric cooperative members encouraging elected officials to keep affordable and reliable electricity at the center of the debate.

When President Franklin D. Roosevelt signed his famous executive order forming the Rural Electrification Administration, he had two goals in mind. First, he wanted to make electricity available to all Americans. And second, he wanted it to be affordable.

Tri-County Electric Cooperative remains as committed to those goals as it was in 1936, when the idea of an electric cooperative was just a dream for many. When the next big anniversary comes along, the cooperative those pioneers built will remain strong thanks to its focus on providing service. As long as people want to live in rural areas, electric cooperatives will be a vital member of the community.

"There is uncertainty in the electricity industry and we see a challenging future," Manager Brian Krambeer said. "It is much like what TEC has seen in the past, but the challenges are different.

"However, through the seventy-five years there has been tremendous commitment and support from members, directors, and employees."

Members of Rushford's Creekside Park Project received a $1,000 donation in 2008 from Tri-County's Operation Round-Up Trust Fund. The money went toward rebuilding the park, which was destroyed in the 2007 flood. Operation Round-Up funds come from members who agree to have their electric bills rounded up to the next highest dollar. The extra change goes into a trust fund and is given to worthy local causes through an application process. Shown here are Park Committee members Jack O'Donnell, Don McCellen, Lisa Ledebuhr, and Phil Gaddis, along with trust board members Rita Baer, Darlene Hrejsa, and Jim Rislow. Children holding the layout of the new park are Mitchell Ledebuhr, Andrea Larson, and Hannah Ledebuhr.

Listing of Board Members

Maurice Tuff (1)	1936–1936
Elmer Tabor (1)	1936–1936
Wilbur Heusinkveld (1)	1936–1936
Fred B. Blanchard (2)	1936–1958
Oliver Haslerud (1) (2)	1936–1940
Laurence L. Tollefson (1) (2)	1936–1937
Nels Byboth (2)	1936–1939
Harry S. Roberts (2)	1936–1938
	& 1948–1961
Guy H. Pierce (2)	1936–1948
Lynn Sheldon (2)	1936–1938
George J. Werner	1937–1948
Mark Corcoran	1938–1942
Edwin F. Luehr	1938–1959
Irving Bacon	1939–1958
Glenn R. Churchill	1940–1967
Edward A. Albrecht	1942–1980
John F. Papenfuss	1949–1976
Arnold C. Schroeder	1958–1968
George F. Mathis	1958–1978
Erling H. Burtness	1960–1978
Arnold H. Onstad	1962–1972
Lloyd M. McKenzie	1967–1976
Elton R. Redalen	1968–1983
Harvey M. Rislow	1972–2002
Paul C. Abrahamson	1976–1989
Ralph R. Frick	1976–1978
Lester F. Unnasch	1978–2000
Naomi R. Fruechte	1978–1984
Jerome A. Gernes	1978–2006
Robert M. Anderson	1980–2005
Judith A. Sikkink	1989–2007
Roger D. Hegland	1983–
Arnold E. Ideker	1984–
T. Allen Aarsvold	2000–
Jeffrey G. Redalen	2002–
Patricia M. VanGundy	2005–
Jennifer A. Scharmer	2006–
Ronald D. Stevens	2007–

(1)   Board Members on January 30, 1936
(2)   Board Members on November 17, 1936

The current board of directors for Tri-County Electric includes, front row (left to right): Arnold Ideker, T. Allen Aarsvold and Jeff Redalen. Back row: Ron Stevens, Patty VanGundy, Brian Krambeer (manager), Jenny Scharmer and Roger Hegland. Photo courtesy of Ross Himlie Photography.

Managers:

Laurence Tollefson (project superintendent), June 1937–December 1937

Oliver Haslerud (project superintendent), January 1938–April 1938

Earl Kjos, April 1938–October 1946

Ray Domini, October 1946–December 1947

George Werner, January 1948–April 1961

Earl Johnson, April 1961–October 1982

Bruce Meistad, October 1982–February 2001

Brian Krambeer, February 2001–present